Transforming
Schools and Schools
of Education

Transforming
Schools and Schools of Education

A New Vision for Preparing Educators

Stephen L. Jacobson
Catherine Emihovich
Jack Helfrich
Hugh G. Petrie
Robert B. Stevenson

In collaboration with
The University Council for Educational Administration
and The Holmes Partnership

CORWIN PRESS, INC.
A Sage Publications Company
Thousand Oaks, California

For information:

Corwin Press, Inc.
A Sage Publications Company
2455 Teller Road
Thousand Oaks, California 91320
E-mail: order@corwin.sagepub.com

SAGE Publications Ltd.
6 Bonhill Street
London EC2A 4PU
United Kingdom

SAGE Publications India Pvt. Ltd.
M-32 Market
Greater Kailash I
New Delhi 110 048 India

LB2165
.T73
1998
0 37418361

Printed in the United States of America

Transforming schools and schools of education : A new vision for preparing educators / Stephen L. Jacobson . . . [et al.].
    p.   cm.
Includes bibliographical references.
ISBN 0-8039-6454-4 (cloth : alk. paper) — ISBN 0-8039-6455-2 (pbk. : alk. paper)
1. Teachers colleges — United States.   2. Teachers — Training of —
United States.   3. Education — Study and teaching (Higher) — United States.
   4. Educational change — United States. I. Jacobson, Stephen L.
LB2165.T73   1997
370'.711 — dc21   97-35717

This book is printed on acid-free paper.

98 99 00 01 02 03   10 9 8 7 6 5 4 3 2 1

Production Editor: S. Marlene Head
Editorial Assistant: Kristen L. Gibson
Typesetter: Judith M. Richards
Cover Designer: Marcia M. Rosenburg

Contents

Preface

In 1988, Clifford and Guthrie published *Ed School*, a sophisticated history and critique of schools of education. By that time, America's public had been exposed to numerous accounts of the failures of public schools. It was only a matter of time until negative attention focused on schools of education. The critique that climaxed in *Ed School* came as no surprise to many of us housed in colleges of education across the nation.

Two organizations had sensed these problems in the mid-1980s: The Holmes Group (serving for a decade as a consortium of research-oriented schools and colleges of education, and now The Holmes Partnership) and The University Council for Educational Administration (UCEA; a 40-year-old consortium of research universities with doctoral programs in school administration). In the early 1980s, these organizations focused their exclusive attention on their respective constituencies of teacher education and school leader preparation. However, by mid-decade there began, under Holmes sponsorship, discussions about a more organic approach to the preparation of education professionals that included Judy Lanier, Harry Judge, and Gary Sykes (representing Holmes teacher education concerns), James Comer (representing the perspectives of education psychology), and Terry Astuto and Patrick Forsyth (representing school leadership and UCEA). These discussions followed Holmes's publication of *Tomorrow's Teachers* but significantly preceded the publication of both *Tomorrow's Schools* and *Tomorrow's Schools of Education*. There was an effort to build a comprehensive coalition that included all of the education professions. That coalition has now been realized in the new Holmes Partnership, but was not operative prior to the publication of *Tomorrow's Schools* and *Tomorrow's Schools of Education*. Holmes went on to produce the second and third volumes of the trilogy independently. However, these discussions did have an effect. There was a clear shift in Holmes's thinking and an acknowledgment of the legitimate concerns for reforming the preparation of school leaders as well as teachers.

This movement toward common ground is also apparent in the activities of UCEA, which began to call for a new emphasis on knowledge and skills related to teaching and learning for school leaders. UCEA's Project on Knowledge and Research in Educational Administration selected teaching and learning as one of the seven domains of knowledge. We have evolved to a position that the various specialties within education cannot continue their myopic preparatory curricula. Teachers, school leaders, and all the professional staff of schools need to know the core technologies of schooling, including teaching, learning, and organizing.

And so it is most appropriate that Holmes and UCEA join forces to publish a chronicle of one school of education's efforts to renew and reshape what it does. We are proud to present this volume, in the hope that it will help, cajole, and affirm the work that others have done or are about to do.

PATRICK B. FORSYTH
UCEA Executive Director

NANCY L. ZIMPHER
President, The Holmes Partnership

References

Clifford, G. J., & Guthrie, J. W. (1988). *Ed school: A brief for professional education.* Chicago: University of Chicago Press.

Holmes Group. (1986). *Tomorrow's teachers: A report of the Holmes Group.* East Lansing, MI: Author.

Holmes Group. (1990). *Tomorrow's schools: A report of the Holmes Group.* East Lansing, MI: Author.

Holmes Group. (1995). *Tomorrow's schools of education: A report of the Holmes Group.* East Lansing, MI: Author.

About the Authors

Stephen L. Jacobson is an associate professor in the Department of Educational Organization, Administration and Policy at the State University of New York at Buffalo. From 1992 to 1997, he was coordinator of the Educational Administration Program and is currently codirector of the Graduate School of Education's Center for Continuing Professional Education. His research interests include the reform of educational administration preparation and practice, teacher compensation, and teacher absence and the social organization of the school workplace. Among his other books are *Educational Leadership in an Age of Reform* (with J. Conway; Longman, 1990), *Reforming Education: The Emerging Systemic Approach* (with R. Berne; Corwin, 1993), and *School Administration: Persistent Dilemmas in Preparation and Practice* (with E. Hickcox & R. Stevenson; Praeger, 1996). In 1994, he was awarded the University Council on Educational Administration's Jack Culbertson Award for outstanding contributions to the field of educational administration by a junior faculty member.

Catherine Emihovich is currently an associate professor in the Department of Counseling and Educational Psychology and the director of the Buffalo Research Institute on Education for Teaching (BRIET) at the State University of New York at Buffalo (UB). Her specializations in research include teacher education reform, integrated services in schools, discourse analyses of children's speech events, and the relationship between culture and cognition. Her most recent book (coauthored with Carolyn Herrington) is *Sex, Kids, and Politics: Health Services in Schools* (Teachers College Press, 1997). She has guest edited special issues of five major journals and was the editor of *Anthropology and Education Quarterly* from 1992 to 1995. She has published or presented more than 50 papers and is currently editing a special journal issue for *Education and Urban Society* on the topic of teen pregnancy as viewed from a sociocultural perspective. In 1995, she received the Distinguished Alumni Award from the Graduate School of Education at UB.

Jack Helfrich is currently a senior fellow and consultant to the Graduate School of Education at the State University of New York at Buffalo (UB). He is also codirector of UB's newly created Center for Continuing Professional Education. Prior to his work at UB, he was superintendent of schools for 13 years in the Kenmore-Town of Tonawanda (Ken-Ton) Union Free School District in New York. During his tenure, Ken-Ton earned numerous state and national Schools of Excellence Awards and, in 1992, it became the first district in New York State to win the governor's Excelsior Award. In addition to the superintendency, other administrative positions he has held during a 40-year career in education include assistant superintendent for curriculum and instruction, director of instruction, high school and elementary principalships, assistant director of a national center in Washington, D.C., and senior staff specialist with the education branch of the Kettering Foundation. These professional experiences have taken him from Puerto Rico to Hawaii with many stops in between.

Hugh G. Petrie is professor of philosophy of education and was dean of the Graduate School of Education at the State University of New York at Buffalo from 1981 to 1997. Active in educational affairs at both national and state levels, he served as the first chair of the Board of Overseers of the Regional Laboratory for Educational Improvement of the Northeast and Islands and was a founding member of The Holmes Groups, now The Holmes Partnership, a consortium of the major research universities and associated schools in the United States devoted to the reform of teaching and teacher preparation. His current research interests center on theories of human action, perceptual control theory, educational policy, ways of knowing, liberal arts and teacher education, organizational learning, and interdisciplinary inquiry.

Robert B. Stevenson is an associate professor and chair of the Department of Educational Organization, Administration and Policy at the State University of New York at Buffalo. He completed his Ph.D. in curriculum and instruction at the University of Wisconsin–Madison. His current research interests focus on practitioner or action research, and the assumptions embedded in policies and programs about how teachers and administrators acquire and use knowledge of educational practice. Previous coedited books include *Educational Action Research: Becoming Practically Critical* (with S. Noffke; Teachers College Press, 1995) and *School Administration: Persistent Dilemmas in Preparation and Practice* (with S. Jacobson and E. Hickcox; Praeger, 1996).

Acknowledgments

The authors would like to thank Gracia Alkema, Patrick Forsyth, and Judith Lanier for seeing the potential of this work and supporting it through completion by their collaborative efforts.

Introduction and Overview

Stephen L. Jacobson

This book is about educational change. It is about change in the field and change at the university. In the chapters that follow, five colleagues examine changes in the ways

1. Schools are governed
2. Faculty in schools of education approach their work and their colleagues in the field
3. Teachers and administrators are prepared and interact in practice
4. Schools and schools of education work with one another
5. Practitioners and faculty conceptualize and utilize research

We argue that if we are to prepare educators to work in the schools of tomorrow, we must do so in tomorrow's schools of education. We envision nothing less than the simultaneous transformation of elementary, secondary, and higher education. It is simply not possible to change any one part of the educational system in isolation of the others. And it is certainly no longer possible for professors of education to advocate reform without participating in such a process themselves.

We recognize fully that many of the changes we propose will be resisted because they threaten traditional power relationships and well-entrenched ways of doing things. Nevertheless, despite resistance, some of these changes have already begun. This book describes a number of pivotal activities that have been undertaken at the University at Buffalo and several school districts in western New York. My four coauthors—Catherine Emihovich, Jack Helfrich, Hugh Petrie, Robert Stevenson—and I have been active participants in these change initiatives, and we have been influenced in our work to a great extent by The Holmes Group trilogy: *Tomorrow's Teachers* (1986), *Tomorrow's Schools* (1990), and *Tomorrow's Schools of*

Education (1995). Individually and collectively, we attended numerous regional and national Holmes Group meetings over the past decade, and Holmes's evolving notion of schools of education working in partnership with schools appealed to us because it mirrored our own efforts at the State University of New York at Buffalo (UB).

We began discussing this writing project shortly after the last Holmes Group National Conference in Washington, D.C., in January 1996—a meeting that focused on the transformation of the Holmes Group into the Holmes Partnership. We thought this period of transition would be a useful time to chronicle our activities so that we could measure where we were as a school of education as compared to where we used to be, and, perhaps more important, where we were as compared to where we would like to be.

This undertaking was intended not only to help provide us with markers of change but also to allow us the chance to reflect upon resistance we have encountered along the way—resistance that sometimes came from others, sometimes came from ourselves, and, upon reflection, sometimes proved to be useful. In addition, the authors' conversation in the last chapter helped us to recognize and discuss where our personal visions about the future converge and conflict. As the reader will see, although many of the changes described in the chapters that follow were clearly interrelated, they were not always well timed or well coordinated. Moreover, the potential success of the simultaneous transformation of schools and schools of education that we advocate will depend, in many cases, on striking an appropriate, dynamic balance between significant but potentially competing needs of key players in the process.

For example, in the first chapter Jack Helfrich describes a long-term school improvement process he initiated when he was hired as superintendent in the Kenmore–Town of Tonawanda (Ken-Ton) Union Free School District. Helfrich found that by allowing teachers and other staff members greater participation in school decision making, leadership emerged from every level of the district. Ken-Ton's new approach to school improvement ultimately proved to be highly successful, earning the district numerous State and National Schools of Excellence Awards and, in 1992, the New York State Governor's Excelsior Award—making Ken-Ton the first school district in the state ever to have earned this recognition. Yet Helfrich's initial attempts at making the district a more collaborative environment were not fully appreciated by a number of principals and senior central office administrators, who were used to exercising exclusive control over the district's decision-making process. Paradoxically, Helfrich found that regardless of what we say about shared decision making, leadership needs to be top-down at times, as in this case, where he had to pressure some of his key administrators into permitting greater staff participation.

Helfrich also reports that, to his disappointment, engaging the university in district reform efforts was no simple task, as his repeated attempts to enlist UB's involvement in Ken-Ton's change initiative went unheeded. Attempting to explain the university's reluctance to engage in these activities, Hugh Petrie reflects on the culture of the modern research university in the second chapter. He contends that although the highly individualized nature of faculty work serves to support their specific research agendas, it may impede faculty involvement in broader educational reform efforts. After he contrasts this traditional university culture with what appears to be an increasing realization that school improvement requires shared visions and the ability to work together, Petrie concludes that a major shift in orientation at schools of education will be needed. He argues that if we are to succeed in placing schools back at the center of practice of schools of education, the right balance needs to be struck between shared visions and the ability to pursue one's own individual goals. By proposing that university faculty begin to move from "my" work to "our" work, Petrie echoes the recommendations of the Holmes Group by encouraging those of us who work in schools of education to reexamine our social contract with public education.

In the third chapter, Catherine Emihovich, explores the implications of organizing a teacher education program around an action research framework. She focuses on what graduate schools of education must do to prepare a new type of professional educator for the field. She argues that we can no longer prepare teachers who follow blindly whatever standards or curricula are handed down from the local, state, or federal level. Instead, we need professionals who can take on leadership roles and make decisions about assessment and instruction, educators who will critique current models and generate models of their own, which in turn can be fed back to the university for testing and refinement, elaboration and discussion. The central question Emihovich raises is: How do we prepare these kinds of educators? In this chapter, she describes the evolution of the Buffalo Research Institute on Education for Teaching (BRIET) preservice teacher training program. Developed initially out of a reflective practitioner model, the preparation of the "teacher as researcher" is now BRIET's central focus.

Emihovich also explores the following key issues:

How do we sustain collaboration over the long haul?

What happens when we involve administrators in school change initiatives?

Who really has the authority to make change happen?

These last questions about collaboration, administration, and authority provide a logical segue into the fourth chapter, in which I argue that leadership preparation provides an excellent basis for university/school district partnerships. Clearly, school districts need to have people with the positional authority to implement change. But just as important is the need for school leaders who have the intellectual and moral authority, as well as the interpersonal skills, necessary to model new ways of interacting with other educators, and these new relationships should be experienced from preparation through practice. To accomplish this transition in how we conceptualize and develop educational leadership, changes need to be made in traditional power relationships that define schools and schools of education. We need to rethink the role of school leaders, whether administrator or teacher, professor or student, if we are to create opportunities for people who have never before been tapped for leadership roles. To this end, I examine three concepts—school as community, collective leadership, and shared vision building—that provide the central underpinnings for the Leadership Initiative for Tomorrow's Schools (LIFTS), a new approach to the preparation of school leaders that has been developed collaboratively by UB and several area school districts.

In the chapter, I also examine resistance to change—resistance that comes from those who feel threatened by these new roles and relationships, including resistance that sometimes comes from ourselves. I conclude the chapter by questioning how we can integrate the preparation of teachers and administrators with that of other school professionals such as school psychologists and counselors. In other words, how do we begin the process of bringing together in preparation those people who will have to work together in practice, and how do we get the various faculties who prepare these individuals to help carry out this transformation?

One of the impediments to how we might work in a more integrated fashion with colleagues in the field and colleagues at the university is the way in which the relationship between research and practice is traditionally conceptualized by both researchers and practitioners. Robert B. Stevenson, in Chapter 5, notes that the dominant approach to research assumes a "top-down" relationship between theory and practice, which is then mirrored in the relationship between university researchers and practitioners. By examining the different roles that research or systematic inquiry can play in the professional lives of practitioners, he provides a framework for thinking about the ways in which they can acquire and use validated knowledge.

Stevenson first describes two ways that educators can use research findings, or the products of research, as (a) guidelines for practice and (b) analytical constructs for thinking about practice. Then he examines two approaches to including practitioners in the research process by using research as (a) a way of co-constructing an understanding of practice (with researchers) and (b) an integral part of their practice. Each of these approaches assumes a different conception of the relationship between research-generated theory and practice. He further argues that although all approaches have a place, the most dominant—using research findings as guidelines for practice—is also the most limited. Therefore, if we are to integrate theory and practice, we need to explore the implications of the other approaches for preparation programs and the role of university researchers. After offering a preliminary exploration of these implications, the chapter concludes by challenging university researchers to create more democratic forms of collaboration in the production of knowledge and action for better schools.

In the final chapter, the five of us discuss the implications of our work for the field and, more specifically, how our chapters can inform activities we are currently engaged in at the Graduate School of Education at UB. This conversation, which took place in mid-December 1996, allowed us to compare our perceptions about the central issues that affect our own work lives, as well as those of our colleagues at the university and in the field. As the discussion evolved, we examined changing conceptions of leadership, including top-down versus participative approaches and the moral dimensions of leadership. We also discussed resistance to change, logistical impediments to program integration, and a general tendency to dichotomize significant reform issues. Finally, we looked at the implications of chaos theory for sustained change and long-term commitment, and the need for organizational stability to help build trust.

Although the five of us have been involved in numerous change initiatives and collaborations over the past few years, we have rarely had the time as a group to sit and reflect about where we see ourselves heading as a school of education with regard to the preparation of tomorrow's educators. We suspect that time for thoughtful reflection is a luxury available to few individuals or programs engaged in similar activities. Therefore, we hope that those involved in or contemplating similar changes in their teacher and administrator preparation programs and their relationship to the field will find our deliberations illustrative and informative.

Recounting key lessons learned from his years of experience in the field, Helfrich notes that school improvement is an inexact science. Over the course of this text, it should be clear to the reader that reform efforts at a school of education are unlikely to be any more precise. Our conversation in the concluding chapter indicates that although we all agree that we can and must make changes in the ways in which our school of education prepares educators and works with the field, we don't always agree about what changes are required or how such changes need to be implemented. Our collective efforts reveal that there is no single formula or one best way to proceed. Instead, change needs to be tailored to the unique situations in each school and school of education. Nevertheless, we hope that the descriptions of our change efforts that follow will help others, particularly educational policymakers, practicing administrators, and university professors, in thinking about their own work. In the end, although this is a story about our school of education and some of its collaborators, it may illuminate the issues all educators face.

1

School Improvement: A View From the Field

Jack Helfrich

This first-person narrative describes 13 years of a school improvement effort I initiated when hired in 1981 as superintendent of the Kenmore–Town of Tonawanda (Ken-Ton) Union Free School District in western New York. With the wisdom of hindsight, I analyze those experiences that I believe were central to initiating change in the district. In this "view from the field," I intend to show that school change is a difficult undertaking that takes time and requires constant renewal. There is no single path to school improvement—in fact, there are many, but all are lined with potholes. Nevertheless, school improvement *can* be accomplished, and the joy of seeing student performance and faculty recognition increase makes it all worthwhile.

During my tenure, Ken-Ton's school improvement process went through a three-phase evolution. The first was a developmental phase that was needed to help the staff overcome its initial reaction to the process, which was "It doesn't work!" I had to ensure that this new initiative would not get bogged down, as did earlier efforts. The second phase of the process focused on building trust and helping district teams involved in shared decision-making activities to realize that they actually had some power. When team members started to feel that they had a voice in the process, their attitude began to change to "It may work!" Finally, by the third phase, the process was defended by the staff because "It works!" During this period, when the process was institutionalized, it was essential to "revisit" and renew our commitment to this collective endeavor to ensure its integrity and to see that teams continued to focus on issues that make a difference in student achievement.

In this chapter, I describe key events during each phase of the process and provide personal reflections about where I thought the district and the staff were at that point in time. To place the discussion in a broader, historical context, I begin with some background information about the school district.

Enrollment Decline and Reductions in Force

In 1971, 10 years before I was hired, the Ken-Ton district had 22,000 students. At that time, western New York had a substantial base of heavy industry and adequate employment opportunities for unskilled and semiskilled workers. Historically, the district had produced excellent student results and had a fine local and statewide reputation. Even when the district's enrollment was one of the fastest growing in the state, and schools faced temporary hardships such as double schedules with large class sizes, staff, students, and parents were proud to be a part of the system. Industrial expansion kept tax rates low, and hundreds of teachers were being hired annually. Central office had grown to the point where desks lined the hallways as there were more administrators than the building could comfortably contain. Even the high school football team was successful, touted to be the best in the nation. But this positive climate started to unravel in the mid-1970s and by 1981, when I was named superintendent, Ken-Ton's enrollment had dwindled to 11,000. Twelve schools had to be closed and more than 600 teachers were laid off. Not surprisingly, these losses had a demoralizing effect on faculty morale. Skewed experience and age demographics produced a very senior workforce, and seniority bumping rights created pockets of unrest, particularly in the district's lowest socioeconomic schools where student needs were greatest. These schools were where the district's least experienced teachers were placed before their eventual layoffs. Yet some of these so-called "young" teachers had almost 17 years of district service and they became cynical and openly hostile toward central office administrators who were about to present them with pink slips. Their anger strained the relationship between management and the union. In fact, the first board of education meeting I attended as superintendent was picketed by the teachers' union, which was then deadlocked in its contract negotiations.

During my first years in the district, the board of education considered teachers the enemy, and teachers felt the same about the board. Because of what teachers perceived as their "slash and burn" tactics during the 3 years before my arrival, central office administrators were viewed as uncaring, brutal lackeys of the board. Grievances were at an all-time high, and any action construed as contrary to the letter and spirit of the contract was immediately contested. There were simply too many negative things happening for building administrators to muster support for school improvement efforts.

Prior Efforts at School Improvement

In 1979, there had been a much-heralded, state-initiated program called Project Redesign that was aimed at launching school improvement efforts throughout the state. Although Project Redesign was generally viewed with skepticism by teachers in the district, it did garner support from some principals and their staffs, who felt that involvement in such a project might help to get their schools back on track. Unfortunately, state financial support for the program disappeared after just 2 years, and so did Project Redesign. Administrators and staff alike were now totally soured on further improvement efforts. Some had been willing to work with the state on Project Redesign, but when they were left to fend for themselves financially for reasons that were never made clear, the state itself became an enemy.

Another obstacle to change had to do with negative faculty perceptions about the superintendency. My predecessor had been hired to do some very tough things: close buildings and downsize the staff. As a result, he was viewed as being relatively heartless and served fewer than 3 years. He had been only the fourth superintendent in the district's history, and the first "outsider." (I would be the second.) Hiring someone from outside the district, from another state in fact, had been traumatic to those who had been in the system for their entire careers. Administrators openly expressed concern about trusting someone who had not come up through their ranks, especially a "hatchet man" charged with reducing staff and closing schools. Some of the most outspoken resistance to building closure came from within the district's administrative ranks, and this negative climate doomed the superintendent. These events and attitudes set the stage for things to come.

Getting Started

To say the least, things were not at their best in 1981. Because of a fiscally conservative school board, funds were tight. Teachers had been receiving only 2% to 3% wage increases, during a period of double-digit inflation, and state financial support was not growing at anywhere near that rate of inflation. No one knew what to do to repair employee relationships, or how to get schools to begin efforts aimed at improving student performance. When I was hired, I confronted two key issues:

1. Was I tough enough to handle the growing conflict?
2. What could I do to get the system back to the business of providing high-quality education?

A subsequent issue, of which I was unaware when hired, was the fact that additional schools were slated to be closed. "Welcome aboard, Jack. By the way, we want you to close four more schools this year!" How could I close four more schools and still build trust? After the failure of Project Redesign, why would administrators support a new school improvement effort? Would the board provide sufficient resources to permit meaningful change efforts? Why would other stakeholders in the district commit to a new program which, at that point in time, had no name, no form, no clear goals? These uncertainties led to many sleepless nights as I considered my options and possible directions.

I realized the district had only a few options:

1. We could do nothing, just let nature take its course. This option I felt was unacceptable.
2. We could bring in an educational "guru" to push the latest "hot" model as the basis for future program development, such as the Madeline Hunter model. But as good a process as that model was, I viewed it as only one element in a broader improvement effort. In my opinion, we could not accept a "one size fits all" approach to school improvement.
3. The last option was to engage all stakeholders—teachers, administrators, parents, support staff, community members, and students—in a change process specifically tailored to the needs of each of the district's schools.

Time, space, students, staff, and materials (in the broadest sense) were the key variables to consider. How we decided collectively to arrange these variables and their interactions would define schooling in the near future. I knew we were in for a long journey with an unclear destination; therefore, one thing we had to avoid was the perception that at some point the process would be completed and we would have "arrived."

Phase 1: It Doesn't Work!

To get the effort started, I explored a number of alternatives. One of my first choices was to engage the university in a partnership. I approached the dean of the graduate school of education (GSE) about the feasibility of a 3-1-3 study program, whereby students would spend 3 years in high school, a transitional year in both high school and college, and 3 years at college earning a degree. We also explored the use of television as a distance-learning instructional link between the university and the high schools. As this discussion took place before the advent of fiber-optic networks and interconnected buildings, it was looked upon by the university's technology people as being too difficult and costly to pursue. It seemed as if their attitude was to find reasons *not* to work together, rather than to develop collaboratively innovative projects that might improve student performance. One major stumbling block for the GSE was that any collaboration with the schools would also require the cooperation of other university units that deal with undergraduate programs. As Petrie notes in the next chapter, cooperative undertakings between decanal units within higher education are no less troublesome than university/school district collaboration. Our initial meeting was also our final meeting and, unfortunately, neither the university nor the district ever followed up on this initiative.

Because there appeared to be no interest on the part of the university to work with a public school system, a second option was to engage an experienced, practice-oriented consulting group for an extended period, perhaps 3 to 5 years. This alternative was selected. The Institute for the Development of Educational Activities (/I/D/E/A/), the educational branch of the Charles F. Kettering Foundation, submitted an intriguing, cost-effective proposal. Their proposal was not prescriptive; rather, it was a developmental process that would involve all stakeholders from commitment to implementation.

The project's initial activity was a 2-day retreat at a local church, a neutral territory. The purpose of the retreat was threefold:

1. To model the types of behaviors that would become the modus operandi of the process itself (e.g., team- and consensus-building activities
2. To give all district stakeholders a chance to discuss important and visceral issues in pursuit of a shared vision
3. To reach consensus about whether stakeholder groups would commit their constituencies to a school improvement process

The retreat ended with a proposal that was endorsed enthusiastically by all participants. It was decided that the project would start with a summer institute to be run by /I/D/E/A/. The institute, the Principals' Inservice Program, would focus on team- and consensus-building decision-making techniques that would be needed in subsequent school improvement programs at each building. As this was one of the first attempts to change an entire district, as opposed to implementing an improvement program at one school within a system, there was little prior experience that could be called upon to move the program forward. This would be a developmental project for /I/D/E/A/, as well as the district.

The summer program was in its third day when there was an inordinate amount of grumbling by the principals in attendance. It became apparent that the district was moving toward site-based management, including the ways that decisions were made. Some principals felt that they might lose power and not be considered the leader of their schools given the cross section of stakeholders who would be involved on /I/D/E/A/ planning teams at each building. Their concern reached a crisis level, and I was informed that principals were not buying into the program. Principals referred to Project Redesign and said that they were wasting their time getting trained for yet another program that would probably be gone in a couple of years.

I called a special meeting of the principals and /I/D/E/A/ consultants. I reminded the principals that their association had committed them to the program, that the board was committed to the program, and that I was committed to the program. Moreover, we had all committed to implementing the program within 3 to 5 years. After a long silence, I told the principals that they had three alternatives available to them:

1. Those 55 years of age or older could retire if they strongly opposed the program.
2. They could help design a program that, if constructed properly, would create an exciting and productive future where all constituencies were involved and focused on one thing—improving student learning.
3. Those principals that might opt to play along but not really commit to the project would have to answer some hard questions about their inability to lead.

This last option was not presented as a real choice, but simply an item for discussion. The meeting had the intended shock value and the summer institute went ahead with less outward rebellion. There were some who were sure that I would topple under the weight of all of the changes being undertaken.

Ultimately, all three alternatives were exercised. There were some retirements, some became excited and worked hard to implement the program, while a few chose to play along, which led to some very difficult face-to-face meetings. In the end, the program was implemented in each of the district's 16 buildings, although with varying degrees of success. Some schools moved ahead rapidly and had two or more facilitators attend both weeklong facilitator training programs run by /I/D/E/A/. Other schools had to be prompted to have individuals attend the training. Some sent staff who were not committed to the program; therefore, their schools gained little from the training, and their planning teams did not deal with any substantive issues during the initial year.

Districtwide support groups were formed so that administrators could meet on a regular basis with /I/D/E/A/ consultants in order to troubleshoot problems. The meetings were designed to focus on and clarify the emerging improvement process. It was often hard to stay focused in the beginning because our collective understanding of the concepts of shared decision making, decentralization, and sharing power was still developing.

That first year was very difficult. The program was in its embryonic stage; there were few individuals who understood what we were attempting, and fewer still who trusted me or /I/D/E/A/. When I met with other superintendents and, occasionally, university faculty, they were often skeptical and even openly derisive of these new ideas. It was nearly impossible to garner support from either group as they had little experience or research to support the program. Our schools were not being "managed" according to prevailing wisdom as presented in course offerings at the university. Superintendents and professors alike joked about the problems that were bound to arise in schools that succumbed to shared decision making.

Redesigning Teacher Evaluation

During that same year, I read the evaluation of every teacher in the district. I was amazed to find that not one had been rated anything other than excellent. With a few exceptions, the evaluations were of little value to teachers or the district. The hard part was coming up with alternatives that would be more meaningful to all parties. The university offered little help, so we again turned to /I/D/E/A/, which had adapted a promising clinical supervision model. A program was designed that would involve all administrators for 5 days during the summer. They would work with classes for gifted and talented students as they worked through the cycle. To help build trust, the union leadership team was invited to participate. I was hoping to demonstrate that this was an inclusive program and that the administration had no hidden agenda.

The workshop was a huge success, and the union leadership was so excited about the process that they requested training for any staff member who volunteered over the next school year. Everyone was astounded when almost half of the faculty went through a modified form of training the following year. This was the beginning of building trust with district staff, a critical element in any successful school improvement effort. For the first time, teachers had an alternative to the formal evaluation process. They could opt for the traditional, 1-page, "green sheet" evaluation, or volunteer to go through a clinical cycle during the school year. If they requested this second option, they could select a clinical team comprised entirely of administrators, or a mix of administrators and teachers, or just teachers. Being able to determine the makeup of one's clinical team further increased the faculty's trust. We were finally on our way to becoming a district involved in improving student and teacher performance, and changing the way business was done. The plan worked exceptionally well and continues to serve the district, having been continuously improved over the years.

This was but one of a number of procedures that have replaced traditional forms of evaluation. The thrust has been to support teachers' efforts to improve and not to simply judge performance one moment in time. The appropriate analogy is that we now use a videotape to document the life of a teacher, not just a series of snapshots.

Teachers as Experts

A second event that contributed to building trust was sending seven teachers to a weeklong conference on learning styles in Madison, Wisconsin. This was the first time in recent history that the district had sent so many teachers so far to enhance their performance. Some teachers with more than 10 years of experience said that this was the first time they had attended a conference at district expense anywhere, let alone out of state. The "Madison Seven," as they came to be known, represented some of our district's best teaching talent. They returned so excited about the possibilities of the "4 Mat" system that they wanted to share what they had learned with any staff member interested and willing to take the time to listen. In the end, it was decided that the team would run awareness sessions for schools interested in this approach to teaching and learning. Most schools opted for the sessions, and so much interest was generated that the program is still being used. The "Madison Seven" became so intensely involved with the material that they met in their homes in the afternoons and evenings to develop their presentations and to further enhance their understanding of the process. This was indicative of the professionalism of the staff and set the tone for future developmental efforts. It is interesting to note that this information came from the private sector and not the university. Again, we were relying on outside consultants rather than institutions of higher education for ideas, help, and support in our effort to improve. During this time, I served on an advisory board to the president of a private college in the area. I suggested that our experiences might be included in an education major's undergraduate methods course. This suggestion was politely noted in the minutes of the meeting and never raised again. Business as usual prevailed.

Reflections on Phase 1

Our school improvement process was starting to take shape. The initial purposes were threefold:

1. To create a 3- to 5-year improvement plan in the form of a shared vision statement
2. To develop an annual plan of realistic goals extracted from the vision statement
3. To create design teams, each responsible for attaining a single goal

These teams would be comprised of individuals who were not members of the planning team but who had expertise in the area of a specific goal

The major achievement of the first phase was getting a disheartened faculty to develop a process that ultimately would be used to elicit a shared vision in all buildings. But getting to that point was not a simple task. As noted at the beginning of the chapter, with the wisdom of hindsight, there are several personal reflections I would like to share.

- Building trust is difficult. Because most perceptions of leadership in the district were based on the actions of my predecessor, creating my own persona took a long time. A leader needs time to build a "track record."
- The leadership style I used with administrators in the beginning was particularly heavy-handed because they had been isolated from central office "leadership" in the past. Setting a different level of expectations was both new and very uncomfortable for the administrators.
- An opportunity for collaboration with the university was missed. The exploration of the 3-1-3 program was short-lived, and their lack of interest led to an increasingly skeptical attitude toward the university.
- When looking for resources to help with staff development, the university again did not prove to be a viable option. There was little precedent and no mechanism to support a university–school system collaboration.

- There was a vast, untapped reservoir of talent in the district capable of providing leadership, especially in matters of curriculum. These potential leaders had always been there, but because administration believed that "important" ideas came from central office and not the staff, this resource was never tapped. Unleashing the talent of these individuals proved to be a powerful tool in building trust.

Phase 2: It May Work!

As a result of our experience with the principal's inservice program, the district invited /I/D/E/A/ to help us develop a school improvement program. The program involved training facilitators, two 1-week seminars, and the creation of administrative support groups that would meet on a monthly basis. Building administrators were divided into two groups so that only one administrator would be gone from a school for any session. Planning sessions for central office staff were held on an as-needed basis.

Initially, one parent and one teacher from each building planning team were sent for facilitator training. Principals and assistants were trained later. We feared that if we trained building administrators first, they would take over the meetings and it would be business as usual. Although this decision created a great deal of unhappiness among administrators, it got the building planning teams off to a good start. After they had gone through facilitator training, principals began to understand how the decision-making process reflected a new, more inclusive philosophy as opposed to the old approach, which excluded voices.

It became evident early in the program that some parents were intimidated by teachers and administrators and that some teachers were intimidated by administrators. People were not used to working with each other and simply did not trust one another. Fear of retribution made many team members reluctant to speak out about issues that might reflect negatively on their school's operation. Meetings did not always go well, and there was some concern that the process was a waste of time as few teams had much to show for their efforts.

It was at this time that two teachers were appointed to the newly created position of districtwide facilitator. These individuals had a genuine interest in the school improvement process, and both had credibility with the staff. They attended planning team meetings regularly in order to help clarify and support the school improvement process. They fostered trust and became expert at helping school teams become productive. Their invaluable efforts

helped us move into the second phase of the process, and the initial successes experienced by planning teams can be attributed in no small measure
to the hard work of these two districtwide facilitators.

As might be expected, the planning teams did not undertake any high-
risk projects during the early years of the program. Risk taking had not been
a part of the district's culture; therefore, few teams were willing to take chances
as they were uncertain of the consequences of failing. Projects to make
cafeterias quieter, renovate rooms, and beautify the school were typical of
initial efforts. Were these endeavors related to improving teaching and learning? Probably not! Were they high risk? Absolutely not! Would they pass
muster in later years? Most assuredly not! However, to have stopped any
one of these initial undertakings would have been the death knell of the
process. To get planning teams to believe that their work actually mattered,
we had to follow through and fund their projects. Getting teams to undertake
high-risk projects that were directly related to the improvement of student
achievement was a gradual process. It took additional trust building and close
to 3 years of work before the teams were actually tackling important issues.

Another thing we learned during this second phase was that the process
had to be revisited on a regular basis if we were to avoid slipping back into
old habits. For example, in the past, a staff development team would be a
standing committee that would simply do a needs assessment. Now we wanted
design teams to pursue programs that would treat staff development as an
outgrowth of an annual plan dedicated to the fulfillment of a shared vision.

It was also during this phase that the administration and union began to
focus on opportunities that would first benefit students and then the staff.
Brainstorming sessions were conducted on a regular basis, not just because
we were negotiating a contract, but because it was satisfying to experience
the evolution of the union-administration culture. The union president was
quite secure in a position he had held for more than 10 years. He was trusted
by the membership and viewed as someone who would do what was best for
staff and students. This was a far cry from the picketing I witnessed at the
beginning of my tenure.

The following is a typical scenario from one of our meetings. In attendance at these informal sessions were the union president and first vice president; the director of personnel, who served as chief negotiator for the district;
and myself. We would usually start with teacher concerns brought to the
union leadership since the last meeting. After those matters were resolved,
one of us might toss out a new suggestion, such as: "Have we ever considered alternative ways of compensating teachers other than basing raises on
an additional year of experience?" The meeting would then become a brain-

storming session, with new and different ideas written on the white board in the office. Many times nothing came of a session other than the seeds of an idea being planted. Yet, at a subsequent meeting, that original idea might begin to grow to fruition. Over my 13 years in the district, many innovative items that ended up in our contract began at one of those meetings.

Planning teams were beginning to rise to the challenge by taking risks and becoming more creative. For example, in one middle school the team felt that some students might be more successful academically if they had more in-depth support from staff. It was proposed that these youngsters be placed in special teams that were smaller than regular teams, and that they receive additional specialized support focused on their particular abilities and disabilities. To accommodate this proposal, some teams would have to be larger than usual because overall staffing would remain unchanged. Nevertheless, the team came up with a plan that was supported by the entire staff. Since this was considered a long-term project, no one anticipated an abrupt change in student performance, but steady improvement was expected. The plan was implemented successfully and the process gained credibility.

At this point, the planning process was modified to enable teams to assess the success of their efforts. Consensus was reached on a proposed monitoring process that would be carried out at the end of each academic year. Monitoring would become an annual activity conducted as a part of the larger planning process. The plan was relatively simple: A monitoring team would create a research design consisting of interviews, questionnaires, or analyses of assessment results. The monitoring process was dependent on the plan developed by the design team, which was, in turn, developed in light of one of the planning team's annual goals, which were derived from the school's vision statement. The process was now complete.

It was also during the second phase that the teachers' union initiated a grant proposal to the state for a teacher center. The proposal, which was supported by both the board of education and the administration, was eventually awarded and received significant state funding. The teacher center was an immediate success, providing support to teachers and the district in areas deemed important by the staff. Many of the courses offered at the center were taught by district teachers and administrators themselves. This had two very positive effects: Recognition and status came with teaching at the center, and those who taught became more expert in the areas they instructed, increasing their value to the system. It was a win-win situation.

The culture of the district was beginning to change. People began to believe "It may work!" Teachers and administrators became vocally supportive and increasingly involved in change efforts related directly to student achievement, even if these efforts were relatively risky. The challenge in the third and fourth year was to keep momentum from faltering. A summer retreat was held to help administrators stretch their imaginations about what the future might hold. The retreat proved to be highly successful. It precipitated further dialogue focused on "what might be," rather than "what is." We began to deal with the future, not just the present. To reflect our belief in collaboration, we expanded this discussion to include representatives from all district schools and departments. Over the years, staff members have come to value these future-oriented presentations and discussions. Individuals were surfacing who were willing to take on leadership roles if they believed an endeavor might produce a more exciting environment and improve student learning.

Planning teams were beginning to mature, and a large number of staff members and parents were trained as facilitators. It was evident that as the number of facilitators increased, so did the district's commitment to the potential of shared decision making and consensus building. Nevertheless, there were still some individuals who did not want to participate in the process, but their numbers grew fewer with each passing year. As more and more staff members witnessed the positive results of their planning, a greater sense of trust and confidence in the process was being established.

One significant error of the initial phase of the process—the omission of support staff from planning teams—was corrected during this second phase. This is a mistake often made by districts involved in change initiatives. There are numerous support staff who have talent and insight as to how schools can be improved, but typically little or no voice in the process. We corrected this oversight by sending a number of support staff members to facilitator training and including them on planning teams. Because nearly half of the district's total workforce are members of the support staff, it made good sense to have them involved and committed to the same vision and goals as teachers, parents, and administrators. In fact, various support staff departments began to create their own planning teams to help improve operations. Planning teams also began including community members who could provide expertise not found elsewhere. They were included in the training component and provided opportunities for leadership in the process. Leadership began to emerge from all levels of the system.

Another error discovered during this phase was the failure to train central office administrators at the beginning of the program. Because they had not been included, many administrators did not understand or trust the planning process. They were suspicious of teams making decisions about issues that were once their sole responsibility, (e.g., hiring new staff). Previously the personnel director would make relatively unilateral employment decisions, and then assign teachers where he felt they would succeed. After school teams were formed, they took over the task of staff selection. They knew their own schools' needs and felt that they could make better decisions as to what strengths and personalities would improve their programs. They now recommended candidates to central office, which worked with those individuals to set salaries and fringes. This was a radical departure from business in the past. It was particularly difficult for some directors who were used to making decisions about who went where. These administrators offered limited support and were openly hostile toward the process. But once we realized the source of their discontentment, central office staff were included in the training process, and subsequently their attitudes tended to improve. As new administrators were hired, they were trained as soon as possible, so they too could become part of the dominant culture focused on improvement.

The circle was now complete. All staff members—including bus drivers, carpenters, groundskeepers, and secretaries—were involved in building planning and development activities at every level. The process was greatly enriched as a result.

Reflections on Phase 2

- Leadership was emerging at every level of the system. Teachers, parents, support staff, and administrators alike were taking on leadership responsibilities, and this new approach to improving schools and student achievement was having a very positive impact on morale.

- Throughout the district, colleagues were learning how to work as equals and to accept and respect the leadership and decision-making abilities of nonadministrators.

- Including support staff increased the success of planning teams. Their inclusion reinforced a culture of change, because now all of the staff were conversant with and involved in the process.

- It was during this second phase that formerly adversarial relationships began to change, becoming more supportive and collaborative. It literally took years to prove that the district was serious about decentralizing decision making and sharing power.

- Excluding central office administrators from facilitator training in the initial phase of the process could have been a fatal mistake had it not been corrected. Sniping by central office administrators could easily have undermined our efforts at decentralization.

- Test data revealed improved student performance subsequent to our change efforts. These results further enhanced the faculty's positive attitude about the process.
- The addition of monitoring to the planning process during this phase proved to be invaluable. Providing planning teams the capability of self-assessment helped them to fine-tune the process.

Phase 3: It Works!

The third phase of the process was to institutionalize the process of continuous school improvement. Although some doubters remained, the process was embraced by the majority of the staff. Conversations in coffee rooms and teachers' lounges were different than when I first arrived. One heard more discussions about improvement efforts and less grousing about problems. The hallmark of this phase was the collective expectation that things could improve if staff members joined in the process of creating a shared vision, and then worked toward achieving that end.

Experience with the process revealed that teams ran into trouble when they mixed problem solving with the vision quest. To keep the two separate, a parallel process was developed to deal with problems only. This was necessary to prevent planning teams from becoming bogged down with day-to-day issues, rather than constructing their collective futures. New groups were formed or existing committees took on the task of problem solving, thus freeing planning teams to focus on future planning. This change in the process, like those before it, took some time because problem solving was the usual approach to improvement in the past.

A related problem was that design teams were becoming standing committees, rather than being reconfigured regularly to address specific goals created in an annual plan. This concern precipitated a call to "revisit" the process. New team members, and some old members who had strayed from the process, were reintroduced to the notion that improvement was not the result of a needs assessment but, rather, that it grows from a planning process based on a shared vision. In addition, there were people who had been on teams since the inception of the program—some who wanted to be replaced and others who needed to be replaced. Long-term team members were perceived as the "in-group," a new elite. This was never the intent of the process, and this perception needed to be dealt with in ways that reestablished the fundamental egalitarian quality of the process. Creative ways of replacing team members evolved in a number of schools, such as inviting visitors to attend meetings for a period of 2 or 3 months. This gave both the team and potential members the opportunity to assess whether they felt strongly enough about the process to become team members. Although other methods were devised, it was rare that term limits were set because the need to achieve annual goals was always paramount over the need to include new and different people.

I encouraged teams to avoid flashy but peripheral issues and focus instead on the primary issue of student achievement. Although this request was easier at this latter stage of development than earlier, it still eluded some teams. In some instances this was due to a lack of leadership, or a lack of understanding, or simply a fear of risk taking. Whatever the reason, if teams were not dealing with maximizing student achievement, then they were reminded to get back to doing those things that make a difference in the larger scheme of things.

Leadership, Focus, and Follow-Through

This brings me back to the importance of focus and follow-through, vis-à-vis leadership. Even though the district was now fully committed to the change process, from time to time it was imperative to step in and refocus planning teams. It was easy for teams to drift from their annual goals to tangential issues of high interest but dubious value. Keeping enthusiasm high and improvement efforts focused was no easy task. Getting into the habit of taking risks and maintaining those efforts had to be monitored regularly. Astute principals would monitor these shifts and refocus their school's team. However, not all principals had the ability or the interest to keep on top of what their teams were doing. When rational discourse failed, other approaches were developed. In some instances, I simply had to make a personal visit to a planning team, or ask the principal and facilitators to submit a plan intended to refocus the efforts of the team. In other instances, mini-retreats were designed to reiterate the team's objective of shared vision. These mini-retreats also provided principals a vehicle to use when teams ran into difficulties in sensitive areas, such as changing teacher behaviors.

Although these might be construed as heavy-handed, top-down managerial techniques, I felt they were necessary to ensure that teams were dealing with issues that make a difference in students' lives and to ensure the integrity of the process. We came to realize that no change model was so perfect that it couldn't benefit from occasional intervention and revitalization. Providing regular opportunities for people to develop and/or renew their understanding of the process offered more and more members of the school community the chance to assume leadership responsibilities. Quite simply, it is necessary to continually reinforce the goals and objectives of the district's school improvement and professional development activities.

Monetary and Psychic Rewards

It was during this third phase that we were able to renegotiate the salary schedules of teachers, administrators, and support staff to reflect the value the district now placed on personal and professional development. Individuals who engaged in activities that enhanced their understanding of our improvement efforts, either through courses at the teacher center or approved graduate courses at the university, received a stipend at the end of the school year. This money was not cumulative; it did not become part of an individual's base salary. If you wanted additional pay, you just needed to engage in professional development activities. These dollar awards replaced some of those that were formerly given as a part of seniority increments.

Additional ways of recognizing staff for their contribution to the district were also pursued. For example, a "Wall of Fame—Staff Development Heroes and Heroines" was established in the community room of the district's staff development building. Because numerous community groups also meet in that room, placing emerging leaders' pictures on the wall provided a great deal of local recognition. Although it seems rather simplistic, this type of acknowledgment was looked upon with great favor by staff members, and getting one's picture on the Wall became an increasingly important motivator for the staff. The Wall of Fame exposed the community to the good work of the district's staff and showed everyone what the district truly valued.

At this time, schools also began applying to Blue Ribbon Schools of Excellence award programs at both the state and national levels. In a 13 year period, 16 schools received the New York State Blue Ribbon School of Excellence award and 7 the National Blue Ribbon School of Excellence award. The board of education honored each of these schools with a recognition dinner and paid for a group of representatives to attend the award ceremonies in either Albany or Washington, D.C. It was clear that the board valued their hard work and the achievements of their students. This further enhanced faculty morale, as noted by a sharp decline in teacher grievances. Pride was back!

When the Governor's Excelsior Award for Quality was initiated, we decided that the whole district should enter. We felt that whatever the outcome, the application procedure itself would be informative because it would provide indicators of what others in the state valued with regard to educational quality. The application was completed by a committee of more than 30 staff members. We were then visited by a team of Excelsior examiners. To our delight, we were the first district in New York State to receive the Excelsior Award. As a result of our receiving this award, district teams, including building and central office staff and members of the board, were invited to make presentations in other districts and at the university, and to participate at meetings about quality education throughout the United States and other countries. The award also precipitated a flood of visitors, which in turn further enhanced staff pride because now *they* were considered "experts" by the field.

I would also like to point out the significant role that members of the Ken-Ton school board played in the success of our efforts. I believe that the school board members in my district were unique relative to usual board standards. When I encouraged them to attend facilitator training in order to gain a better understanding of the school improvement process, most did. Their participation enhanced their knowledge and understanding of the day-to-day operation of schools and encouraged them to become members of district planning teams. Because they were now part of the process that initiated various requests for resources, they were able to spend less time questioning the need for those requests. Having board members advocate the process at public meetings was a real plus. It helped build trust and credibility with the staff and the community. Also unique among boards of education, at least in my opinion, was the way this board changed its perspective about educational policy. In the past, policies were implemented, for the most part, to prevent people from doing things. Now policies were developed to support and facilitate the process of school improvement, not to impede it.

Collaboration With the University

One other activity of note began during this third phase at a regular meeting of area school superintendents. A superintendent from a neighboring district expressed concern about the poor quality of candidates being interviewed for administrative openings in his district. His concerns were mirrored by those of other superintendents at the meeting. A meeting was set up with the dean of the Graduate School of Education, faculty from the university's educational administration program, and representatives of four local school districts. Together, the districts and the university designed an innovative program to prepare a pool of high-caliber leaders capable of facilitating the type of ongoing school improvement effort described in this chapter. The program was called the Leadership Initiative for Tomorrow's Schools (LIFTS), and it began in the summer of 1994. (LIFTS is described in more detail in Chapters 2 and 4 by Petrie and Jacobson, respectively.)

This truly collaborative effort was staffed by practitioners from the public schools, as well as professors from the university. The LIFTS model was seen as a real breakthrough by many local superintendents. Complementing work begun with two other area districts by BRIET (the Buffalo Research Institute on Education for Teaching, an innovative teacher preparation program described in greater detail in Chapter 3 by Emihovich), the implementation of LIFTS indicated that the university was ready to collaborate with public schools in western New York in a meaningful attempt to address their needs.

In the eyes of superintendents, this was finally an opportunity to have access to the resources and expertise of the university to deal with issues important to the field. Such a collaboration was one of the goals enumerated by The Holmes Group. Yet getting support for leadership development is not always easy. Even though they bemoan the fact that the pool of potential candidates is weak, some boards of education, and even some superintendents, are reluctant to invest in leadership development in times of tight money and high public scrutiny. I should point out that some of these same districts claim that they consider staff development a high priority, yet they fail to place the same importance on the development of school leaders. I believe that this is an issue that needs immediate attention from both the university and the field. Over the long term, the generalized staff development efforts in schools will only be enhanced by greater attention to leadership development of teachers and administrators.

Reflections on Phase 3

By the third phase of the process, more and more of the staff were willing to take the lead on risky projects, and fewer were worrying about job security. More and more of the school teams remained focused on important issues rather than drifting off onto peripheral items. Principals, central office administrators, and school board members had a better understanding of the process than during earlier phases. As a result, they were more supportive of each school's pursuit of its annual goals. The recognition gained through state and national School of Excellence awards proved to be a powerful incentive for staff to continue working on the improvement process.

As superintendent, I was viewed as the "keeper of the vision"—the individual who would maintain the integrity of the process and keep it focused on student performance. This required providing resources to support professional development and encouraging teams at each school to increase their expectations of student performance. With an eye to the future, I was delighted that school district/university collaboration was finally being developed around a preparation program for a new generation of school leaders.

After having worked with the process for a number of years, it had become apparent to most in the district that school improvement *is not* a "silver bullet," wherein a one-shot workshop or presentation would fix everything. Although this myth had persisted among some of our administrators, with time they too began to realize that the failure of such programs was due to inability to sustain and support staff efforts. Because it is based on changing the way people think and act, school improvement *is* a dynamic, long-term process that requires constant effort and nurturing. Make no mistake about it, school improvement is difficult.

Conclusion

To hopefully make the journey of others a little smoother, I offer a few final observations.

- Educators have little experience with and knowledge of group processes, even though we purport to be using them in classes and so forth. We need to train people in a process if it is going to be successful. We need a common vocabulary, a common understanding, and, if a process needs to be changed, a vehicle that will help us do it.

- Regardless of how much effort, time, and money we put into the process, there will be failures along the way. But if these experiences are viewed as learning experiences, then the process and the program will continue to improve.

- At times, leadership may need to be top-down, particularly if the process is in jeopardy. Sometimes someone has to take over and get the ship back on course, someone who understands what the goals are and what needs to be done to keep things moving toward those goals.

- Leaders need to be increasingly willing to shift decision making to the appropriate teams. They have to let these teams make decisions and then be supportive of their decisions.

- Improvement is an inexact science. There is no formula for success. It is developmental in nature and must be tailored to the unique situations in each school. Since each site is different, the process has to take that into account and weave these differences into the cloth of change.

- If given the chance, leadership will emerge from all segments of the staff. Watching this transpire was, perhaps, the most gratifying of my experiences over the course of those years.

Currently, the change process is poorly understood by administrators in most school systems. Leadership in public schools can no longer be viewed as solely within the domain of administration. Administration must deal with "the here and now," whereas leadership must be concerned with the future. If schools are to improve to the point where all students are performing at world-class levels, they must prepare for the future and not keep trying to fix an outmoded model. Our public schools and universities must prepare future leaders who understand this critical difference between administration and leadership—leaders who know how to bring about change. We need to work together to get the job done.

Over the course of 13 years, the process we developed at Ken-Ton became the district's accepted way of effecting school improvement. The process was valued highly by the staff because they played an integral role. When I announced my intention to retire, concerns arose about the future leadership of the district, concerns that would only heighten if the union president were to retire soon thereafter. There was speculation that the process might be in jeopardy if a new superintendent, with a different approach to school improvement, was hired. When these concerns were voiced, the board was quick to respond that the process was so important to the district that it would continue to be used in improvement efforts by the new administration. They also pointed out that a fresh perspective could prove helpful in determining new directions for the district's schools. After a careful search, the board hired a superintendent who was willing to commit to the school improvement process, and, soon after, an assistant superintendent for instruction who had formerly been an employee of /I/D/E/A/ and was thus knowledgeable about and committed to the process.

However, at the May 1997 Ken-Ton school board elections, one of the strongest supporters of the school improvement program was defeated by a candidate who either did not understand the process or was unsupportive of it. This new board member has, in the past, raised objections to the costs of staff development and the amount of time spent on planning. Therefore, it is unclear what direction the board will take in the near future. But, even if the board proves supportive, the question still remains: Can a process become institutionalized when the chief executive has not been a part of its development? It is hard to say. I believe there is a need to bring new administrators up to speed in the operation of the process. This is equally true of new members of the board of education. If they lack an understanding of the process, they might ignore effective programs and exhort a new superintendent to get something new going, just to break the link with the past. This would be unfortunate, inefficient, and very expensive, as a considerable investment of time, effort, and money in developmental efforts would go to waste. It is my sincere hope that continuous improvement remains the district ethos and that the process will become even stronger than before. Time will tell.

2

From "My Work" to "Our Work"

Hugh G. Petrie

Several years ago, the American Association for Higher Education (AAHE) sponsored a conference from which I have shamelessly stolen the title of this chapter. From a number of conversations with Russell Edgerton, former president of AAHE and current Education Program Director of the Pew Charitable Trusts, I know that he is very concerned with the tendency of American higher education to become even more of an ivory tower, unconnected with the world, than the popular caricatures would have it. One of the key issues, in Edgerton's thinking, is the faculty culture, especially in research universities, of viewing themselves as more or less independent intellectuals who happen to have a mailing address and electronic mail account at a well-known, or less well known, research university.

Interestingly, this phenomenon extends to some degree beyond the research university to the regional colleges and universities and the liberal arts colleges—both public and private. The reason is not hard to fathom. Even if a given institution aspires to something other than being a research university, its faculty have all been prepared at doctoral-granting research universities. It is very hard for these faculty to give up what they learned as graduate students at the knees of their mentors.

What I am talking about here is very familiar to those who work and study in the academy. Indeed, it is captured in the very language we use. We speak, for example, of teaching "loads" and research "opportunities." When asked to serve on a curriculum committee, faculty sometimes decline, citing such problems as a contract to get "my" book done. Vacations and summers are viewed as the time to focus on "my" work; there is never enough time during the regular academic year. Even advising doctoral students is sometimes viewed as interfering with "my" work. "How will I ever get tenure if I don't publish?"

And, of course, institutions contribute to this culture. They endorse a "publish or perish" mentality, although arguably with more attention to teaching these days. Most of the academic rewards appear to accrue to those who are publishing scholars, especially those who obtain outside grants, thereby enabling themselves to "buy out" of teaching. (Only recently has it become even thinkable for some faculty to "buy out" of research obligations, possibly with more or better attention to teaching.) Even more insidious are the subtle ways in which promotion and tenure and merit salary increases are determined. In most, if not all, disciplines, joint research is looked upon with some skepticism. "How can we tell if Professor X is an independent scholar?" "How much of this is due to the coauthor?" "Our work," even in the field of scholarship, to say nothing of our work in building an outstanding preparation program or jointly teaching a course, or a block of courses, or in building a faculty mentoring and advising system for students, is at least suspect, if tolerated at all.

Yet, as some in higher education are beginning to realize, this single-minded commitment to individual scholarship, although it may have benefits in the occasional intellectual breakthrough, has, for the most part, effectively neglected other functions of the modern university (Boyer, 1990). The community of scholars cannot be simply those folks across the country who are pursuing the same esoteric scholarship (Jencks & Riesman, 1969) no matter how much the Internet allows this community to flourish. A portion of "our work" must come to include what we do locally in preparing students in general education, in an academic major, and for professional roles outside the academy; and providing continuing educational opportunities for our many constituencies. Society is no longer willing to grant carte blanche to higher education to be a haven for independent scholars, each pursuing her or his individual work.

Nowhere is the imperative to shift our effort from "my work" to "our work" more needed than in schools of education. Several treatises over the past decade or so (Clifford & Guthrie, 1988; Holmes Group, 1986, 1990, 1995; Judge, 1982) have pointed out the disconnection between many schools of education and the constituencies they nominally are intended to serve. Too often, many faculty in schools of education, especially those in the policy and social and psychological foundations areas, tend to view themselves primarily as ersatz scholars in the liberal arts and sciences disciplines with only a modest responsibility for professional education. Even those faculty in the curricular areas, such as reading or mathematics education or administration, although they may feel a connection to professional educators, seldom work jointly with each other to see how their varying preparation programs do, or do not, fit together to prepare educational professionals for work in real schools.

Thus, the collaborative efforts called for by the other writers in this book, as well as a vast array of commentators across the country, are severely threatened by the "my work" culture that still prevails in the modern university. Collaboration is tough work under the best of circumstances, to say nothing of a situation that expressly seems to encourage the exact opposite.

In this chapter, I will describe from my perspective—as a dean of a school of education in a research university for 16 years—some of the efforts we made, both successful and not so successful, to begin the journey from "my work" to "our work." I will talk about collaboration within the school of education, with the field, and with other segments of the university. I will also make a few impressionistic observations about the need to shift from "my work" to "our work" within the schools themselves. Indeed, in its way, the isolation of individual teachers within their own classrooms is every bit as much an example of "my work" taking precedence over "our work" within the school or district as is the individual research work of the university professor.

Then I will briefly explore just how "our work" in education might be construed and how we might determine just what our work might be. I will discuss the need to find a proper balance between "my work" and "our work" and how we might begin the process of reaching that balance. Finally, in light of "our work," I will suggest the need to reconceptualize some of our most cherished educational ideals—the generalizability of research, the nature of research findings in professional fields such as education, accountability, and the prospects for "going to scale" with educational reforms.

Our Work in the University

There have been three major areas in which I have tried to encourage thinking about our work at the State University of New York at Buffalo (UB)—within the school of education, with the arts and sciences, and with the field of professional educators. As has happened with a number of Holmes Group institutions, the easiest and, perhaps, most successful area has been in encouraging relationships with the field, and the least successful has been with the arts and sciences and, to some extent, within the Graduate School of Education.

Relations With a Local District

However, even in our relationships with the field, the sailing has not been at all smooth. In Chapter 1, Jack Helfrich described his early attempts while superintendent of a local school district to connect more with me at the Graduate School of Education and more generally with the University at Buffalo. The early contacts with the school of education looking for help with staff development were largely unsuccessful, at least in part because that kind of activity has traditionally been conceived by education faculty members as part of their personal work, leading on occasion to individual consulting arrangements, but seldom as part of their university work. Indeed, it has taken a dozen years for the Graduate School of Education to establish a Center for Continuing Professional Education charged specifically with bringing our resources to bear on the kinds of initiatives Helfrich approached us about in the early 1980s. Ironically, Helfrich, after he retired from the superintendency, became the first director of the center.

The difficulties Helfrich had with the 3-1-3 proposal illustrate both the problems we in education have in communicating with our arts and sciences colleagues and the difficulties they have in communicating among themselves. A 3-1-3 program of 3 years of high school study, 1 year of simultaneous high school and college study, and 3 years of college study is largely the responsibility of the university as a whole, not the school of education. However, the schools have typically had their best relationship, however questionable, with schools of education and not with the rest of the university. Furthermore, at UB, we have had a decades-long struggle with how best to coordinate general undergraduate study. We were then organized with three decanal units in the arts and sciences—arts and letters, social sciences, and natural sciences and mathematics—with great difficulty in locating overall responsibility for undergraduate education. To whom could I have referred the school to discuss the 3-1-3 program?

The question of pursuing such general academic relationships with local schools has recently reemerged with several other school districts. However, the difficulties of coordination among the various aspects of the arts and sciences at the university remain. Interestingly, another barrier related to just what "our work" consists of has become apparent. It is very difficult for high school teachers and university faculty in, say, mathematics to agree on what their joint work is with respect to teaching mathematics. The university faculty are suspicious of the capability of high school teachers to provide appropriate instruction in college-level courses (despite the fact that many high school teachers moonlight in our evening division teaching college courses). For their part, teachers in the schools and especially school board members are suspicious of the capacity of university faculty to provide decent teaching experiences for their high school seniors. Just what "our work" might look like in that 1 year of a 3-1-3 system is highly debatable.

From the Faculty of Educational Studies to the Graduate School of Education

When I became dean of the State University of New York at Buffalo (UB) in 1981, the organization for which I had responsibility was called the Faculty of Educational Studies. As I became aware of the history of this somewhat unusual name, I found that there were at least two major reasons for it. First, the use of "Faculty of" instead of "School or College of" as descriptive of the major units of the university derived from the heady days of the establishment of the old private University of Buffalo as one of the university centers of the new State University of New York. Martin Meyerson and Warren Bennis conceived of the organization of this new venture in ways that they hoped would encourage innovative, interdisciplinary modes of operation, and one way of signaling this intent was to call the major units faculties instead of schools or colleges. The three separate faculties—of Natural Sciences and Mathematics, of Social Sciences, and of Arts and Letters—are only now being combined into a single College of Arts and Sciences.

However, in the case of the professional units, there was some discussion over whether they should be known as "faculties" or as the more traditional "schools." In the end, many became faculties and a few retained the more traditional school appellation. In education, I am told, the decision was clear. If the traditional arts and sciences were to be faculties, so also should education be a faculty. It was a classic case of education feeling like a poor relation and attempting to ape the perceived status of the arts and sciences (Clifford & Guthrie, 1988). An additional reason had to do with the degree structures in education at UB. We offer no undergraduate degrees in education—only masters and doctoral degrees, along with a small, highly selective teacher education certification sequence for UB undergraduates and masters students who have had no previous education experience. Thus, we traditionally have had relatively little to do with beginning teachers.

Over the course of time, several of the professionally oriented units changed their names back to schools and a few years after my assuming the deanship, the provost asked the three remaining professional units that still had "Faculty" in their titles—law, education, and engineering—whether or not they should be schools. Law and engineering changed, I understand, fairly easily. In education, however, the debate raged for nearly a year. Some of the faculty (small "f") asked what the fuss was about. A rose by any other name would smell as sweet. Most, however, took the possibility of a name change very seriously and asked what it would imply for our status in the university. Would we become just another Buffalo State College doing nothing but training teachers? (Buffalo State is another SUNY unit, State University College at Buffalo, whose historical mission had been as a normal school, preparing large numbers of beginning teachers.)

There was additional concern because the question of a name change was occurring at the same time that I had been pushing The Holmes Group's agenda for taking teacher education seriously and improving our relationships with the field of education. Was this just another way for the dean to devalue "real scholarship" (read "my work")? If we became a school, would this mean that we would actually have to deal seriously with teachers and administrators and counselors and psychologists and not just with reproducing ourselves as professors of education through our doctoral students?

This was no idle debate. Consider for a moment the connotations of "Faculty of Educational Studies." First, a faculty would be coequal with the arts and sciences wherein lie the paradigms of university scholarship and the source of the traditions of "my work." Second, and perhaps more important, the name implied that we would "study" education, not necessarily get our hands dirty actually trying to improve it. As studiers of education we could distance ourselves from the actual day-to-day problems of education and schools and need assume little or no responsibility for the actual profession. We would not have to see educational reform as "our work" in the sense that we would be identified with the educational professionals in the field. "My work" would at most be to study the work of educators, critique it, but certainly not be contaminated by it.

Indeed, one of the most often-repeated concerns during the debate on the name change had to do with the extent to which in becoming a school of education we would become so closely identified with the field that we would have to take our scholarly problems as the field presented them. This, it was argued, would cause us, thereby, to lose our independence as scholars and critics of education. There was a great fear of becoming too closely associated with the field, of seeing "our work" as almost solely determined by the profession of education rather than the scholarly disciplines and traditions.

Indeed, these reactions were not surprising. They came from an understandable mix of wanting to protect one's own turf where one felt comfortable; from ego involvement in that turf; from informal membership in a collective that gives the rewards for traditional scholarship—a collective that, for the most part, does not include practicing professionals; and from a real concern that the quality of the academic enterprise might be seriously threatened. After all, the quality standards on which university faculty are born and bred seldom include reference to any other than the narrowly defined community of scholars from higher education.

In the end, however, enough faculty became convinced that within any professional field there could be radical critics who, nonetheless, were clearly committed to the field. In some instances, it would be possible to have closer connections to one's profession without automatically assuming that the ways in which that profession defines its problems are the most useful ways to look at things. One could be an academic in a professional school without losing one's independence of thought. The possibility of applying a more Deweyan standard of quality in terms of the actual outcomes of one's work (Dewey, 1929/1960) could be seriously entertained. In this way we finally agreed in 1989 to change our name from the Faculty of Educational Studies to the Graduate School of Education. "Our work" now at least had the possibility of embracing the real problems of our colleagues in the profession.

The Buffalo Research Institute on Education for Teaching (BRIET) and the Leadership Initiative for Tomorrow's Schools (LIFTS)

As noted above, the discussion of the name change occurred during a period of recommitment to the field in general. The Graduate School of Education (GSE) at UB was generally intrigued by the emerging Holmes agenda to reemphasize teacher education. Indeed, I served as one of the founding members of the board of directors of Holmes and was its first vice president of the northeast region. Nevertheless, the faculty of GSE were never quite sure that they wanted to adopt the Holmes "model" as their own, and because I never conceived of Holmes as offering a highly prescriptive model; this was fine with me. Instead, GSE engaged in lengthy discussions to determine how the important early insights of Holmes could best be implemented at UB.

The first effort in this direction was the establishment of BRIET. Before BRIET, there was a very small Office of Teacher Education. It consisted of one faculty member on a part-time administrative assignment and a secretary. The director of the Office of Teacher Education cajoled chairs into offering the courses needed for the initial certification sequence, and when this did not work, approached the dean to hire temporary instructors to teach the foundations and methods course. Teacher education was, as was true in many institutions at the time, very much of a low-status enterprise in a traditionally low-status academic field (education) attempting to gain status by distancing itself from a low-status, feminized profession (teaching).

BRIET took over the responsibility for our existing teacher education certification sequence, but, more importantly, it conceptually and practically married the traditional responsibility for teacher education with research and scholarship. This marriage was reflected in its very name. This was the only way in which teacher education could reasonably be seen as part of the culture of the university. Another small step had been taken. "My" scholarly work might now be a part of "our" work to improve teacher education.

One of the most interesting features of the establishment of BRIET was the institution of the Clinical Faculty Program (Cornbleth & Ellsworth, 1994). The program involved extensive negotiations with two local school districts, one urban and one suburban, and their respective teachers unions. The program that emerged established a system of clinical faculty closely involved with our teacher education program and working 10-plus hours per week with us on it. These clinical faculty played a variety of roles, from teachers of some methods courses to researchers into their own teaching to major actors in the redesign of the teacher education program. There were many missteps (cf. Cornbleth & Ellsworth, 1994; Ellsworth & Albers, 1995) and we still do not have it all right, but it is clear that we are now much closer to seeing teacher education as "our" work where the "our" encompasses not only university faculty but outstanding area teachers and administrators as well. Indeed, true to its name as the Buffalo Research Institute on Education for Teaching, "our" work was seen not only as the collaborative preparation of teachers, but as joint research on teaching and teacher education as well. The first major research project undertaken by BRIET was on the "wisdom of practice," and current work extends that collaborative thrust with the theme of "teacher as researcher." "Our work" includes both school and university faculty teaching together and researching together.

This new spirit of collaboration spawned a few years later an even more intensive form of collaboration between the field and the GSE. The superintendent of one of the districts cooperating in the BRIET program came to us, and, with the support of several of his Western New York colleagues, posed a challenge to the GSE. He observed that most districts in western New York were about to face a major round of retirements among their administrative staffs. Furthermore, although there were frequently hundreds of nominally certificated applicants for each administrative opening, there were very, very few who were truly qualified. What, if anything, could the university do to help?

Our answer was to design collaboratively with the administrators in the field an extraordinarily innovative leadership preparation program called LIFTS, for Leadership Initiative for Tomorrow's Schools (see Chapter 4). The program does not focus on administrative roles and responsibilities as these are traditionally conceived but, instead, speaks of preparing leaders. We recognized early on that many of the leaders of tomorrow's schools might well not be administrators in the traditional sense. In addition, instead of relying on self-selection, the students are nominated by the districts and jointly selected for the program by school and university faculty. The students attend as a cohort, and because of the early identification of potential future leaders, common in business and industry but virtually unknown in education, arrangements are made to heavily subsidize the participants in the 2-year program. This allows the students, who are typically midcareer professionals, to take time off from their work without major personal sacrifices. Interestingly, this pre-identification feature has caused some controversy in that it is viewed by some as a way of enshrining the status quo. Indeed, without careful attention to selecting truly promising candidates, the program could degenerate into picking the superintendent's favorites.

LIFTS is field based and problem oriented. There is a significant amount of fieldwork, and the curriculum is organized around problems that are then used to bring to bear the knowledge found in more traditional, course-oriented preparation programs. LIFTS also builds on the collaborative successes piloted in the BRIET Clinical Faculty program, and the responsibility for each LIFTS cohort is shared by university and field personnel.

One of the more interesting developments has been the incorporation into the LIFTS program of the /I/D/E/A/ group process work described in Chapter 1. This work has come to be seen as one of the most important components of the LIFTS program. It is highly unlikely that the university would have picked up that portion of the curriculum had not "our work" in leadership preparation been conceived as involving both university and school personnel.

Some Problems

BRIET and LIFTS are at least partial success stories. They illustrate, along with the acceptance of GSE's role as a real professional school, the expansion of "my work" to include significant interactions with the field. For many faculty "our work" now includes this collaboration with professional educators, especially in preparation programs, but increasingly for some in research activities as well.

But even with BRIET and LIFTS there is still probably more collaboration with the field than there is across segments of the GSE. Although, for example, our teacher preparation programs require various courses in the psychological and social foundations of education and these courses are typically well taught and well received, the foundations professors do not really see themselves as teacher educators.

More interestingly, although BRIET has encouraged relationships with the field and has even stimulated some research activities on teaching and teacher education, it has also tended to provide an excuse for significant numbers of professors in the teaching fields (e.g., science, mathematics, elementary education, and reading) to pay less attention to initial teacher preparation and concentrate instead on work at the master's and doctoral levels. (New York State requires a master's degree for permanent teacher certification, but beginning jobs are obtained with essentially bachelor's level preparation.) It still takes nearly constant jawboning by the dean and chairs to ensure that regular tenure-track faculty teach the beginning methods courses, and a recent retreat on the curriculum for our beginning teacher education sequence drew very few professors from the teaching fields.

Even within well-defined master's and doctoral programs, the mathematics education professors, for example, see themselves as having little in common with the science education professors and even less with the reading professors. To be fair, this has recently been changing with the natural emergence of a language and literacy group encompassing professors of reading, language education, English education, and early childhood education. A mathematics, science, and technology group also appears to be forming, in part in response to the state of New York grouping those areas together in its new curriculum frameworks. "Our work" expands only grudgingly.

A second example of the qualified nature of even our success stories has to do with the LIFTS program. By all measures, external and internal evaluations, student and employer response, and the reactions of those who teach in the program, LIFTS, now working with its third and fourth cohorts, is an outstanding success. Nevertheless, the tensions with those who teach solely in the more traditional program are considerable. We have yet to determine if LIFTS is just an experiment carried on by a few or will become "our way" of preparing educational leaders in the future.

Integrated Professional Preparation Programs

One of my more fascinating experiences as a dean occurred a half dozen years ago when I had a meeting of the program directors in the traditional teaching fields, administration, counseling, and school psychology. I observed that each of them was engaged in preparing professionals for work in the institution we call "school." Out in the real world their graduates would increasingly have to interact with each other as site-based management became more common and the school as the site for community services increased in importance. I wondered what each of them did to help their graduates learn to interact professionally with the other role-groups working in schools. Indeed, I wondered what each of them actually considered a "school" to be and asked them to share with each other. There was an embarrassing silence.

Since that time the notion that "my work" in preparing certain professionals for schools and other educational agencies might have interesting connections with "your work" in preparing different professionals for work in those same institutions has become much less threatening. We now talk about the need for integrated professional preparation programs, and some preliminary continuing professional development work is occurring between several faculty associated with BRIET and with LIFTS. Nevertheless, we are still barely at the threshold of conceiving of "our work" as that of collaboratively preparing professionals to work in schools (but see Knapp et al., 1993). After all, the curriculum is already full, with much of it mandated by the state and external agencies. We could not reasonably add something to help our students interact better with each other, and we certainly would have a difficult time leaving anything out. That, after all, would be a threat to "my work." So we struggle on.

Relationships With the Arts and Sciences

At UB the notion that the preparation of educational professionals might involve more than the School of Education is one that yet has to take hold in the minds of very many faculty or administrators in the arts and sciences. Part of this inability of liberal arts faculty to see education as part of their work is easily understandable. Our very small teacher certification sequence (about 100 students per year with only about 40 of them UB undergraduates) is simply not large enough for the arts and sciences faculty to take very seriously.

More disturbing, however, are the reactions of arts and sciences faculty to the occasional news story bashing education. They cluck disapprovingly at the low standards of teacher education. However, when I point out that far and away most of the education that teacher candidates receive comes from them and that low scores of teacher candidates on tests of general knowledge and content can most plausibly be traced to their courses, they stare at me uncomprehendingly.

To be fair, at UB (as, I suspect, at most research universities) every department in the arts and sciences tends to have one or two faculty who take teaching seriously and who are interested in improving the lot of teaching in the schools, although usually only in the secondary schools. Elementary education continues to be a huge mystery to even the most sympathetic arts and sciences faculty. It is these few faculty who take teaching seriously with whom we in GSE have tried to interact with some very modest successes.

Two projects deserve special mention. Early on, UB was one of the members of the Project 30 Alliance. This Carnegie Corporation–sponsored enterprise specifically attempted to involve education faculty with arts and sciences faculty around several themes that clearly call for the participation of the liberal arts in improving teacher education. These themes were

1. The teacher's subject matter
2. Entitling the teacher as professional (general knowledge)
3. Pedagogical content knowledge (how to teach specific content)
4. Minority participation in teacher education
5. International and multicultural perspectives

The Project 30 experience at UB was an interesting one. It brought together about a dozen or so liberal arts and sciences and education faculty who interacted around several issues peculiar to UB. It also was the stimulus for my own participation with a Distinguished Teaching Professor of Biology, observing how he provides extremely extensive teaching experience for both graduate and undergraduate teaching assistants in his courses (see Petrie, 1992, for a report of this experience).

However, in the long run, the project at UB eventually collapsed. We simply did not need it in order to maintain and even improve our small teacher certification sequence. Furthermore, the other projects that were stimulated through the Project 30 meetings seemed to be able to continue without the help of Project 30. One would have to say, I suppose, that very little progress was made toward moving from "my work" in either education or the arts and sciences to "our work" together.

A second project was the New York State American History Academy. This was one of a small number of federally funded projects during the Bush administration to improve the content knowledge of secondary school teachers. Using some of the contacts made through Project 30, a very interesting collaborative project involving education faculty, history and American studies faculty in the arts and sciences, and high school teachers from across the state was put together. Probably the most salient feature of the project from my point of view was that it explicitly set out to involve all the participants as colleagues. The university people were not simply going to "deliver" the truth, Lady Bountiful–like, to the poor, benighted secondary teachers. Instead, all participants were treated as colleagues, and the university faculty learned as much about teaching history as the secondary teachers learned about new views of history. Except for the fact that the project disappeared after the external funding disappeared (so what else is new?), the American History Academy probably really did exemplify concrete steps toward viewing the teaching of history as the collaborative work of education professors, historians, and secondary teachers.

From "My Work" to "Our Work" in Schools

In Chapter 1, Helfrich wrote a good deal about the changes that can sometimes occur in schools within a progressive school district to help everyone come to see the education of the children as their work. However, in my experience, the process he described is all too unusual. More often, one has the teachers in one camp, the administrators in another, the parents suspicious of both, and the pupil personnel specialists—the counselors, psychologists, and health service professionals—hovering around the edges.

The one area in which there appears to be some real progress in schools, especially where some form of site-based management is in effect, is in teachers' and administrators' seeing their joint task as that of promoting student learning. Indeed, in ways similar to our LIFTS program, more and more schools are seeing the leadership in a district diffused across a number of traditional roles. Teachers are taking on increased responsibility in the staff development areas, in working as mentors for new teachers, and, on occasion, helping an institution of higher education with its teacher education programs.

Teachers are also beginning to move from their individual work within their closed classrooms to joint cooperative work across classrooms. Grouping teachers with joint responsibility for numbers of students, sometimes for a several-year period, is one way of tapping the benefits of teachers working together. Much is happening in this area. More needs to be done.

A highly contentious area in some school districts is the extent to which parents and teachers see their individual work with children as "our work." Much rhetoric is expended on the need for teacher-parent collaboration, but the actual results tend to be meager and inconsistent. This is especially so in many urban areas where parent groups persistently complain about the unwillingness of teachers to work with them. Conversely, teachers in urban areas fairly consistently cite the lack of interest and involvement in their children's education on the part of many urban parents. Clearly, this is a fruitful area for increased attention.

Another interesting possibility is for students to see themselves as involved with teachers and parents in the joint work of their own learning. Too many students—urban, rural, and suburban—tend not to view their own learning as at least in part their responsibility. They sit passively, daring the teachers to interest them in anything, let alone teach them something. As we learn more and more about active learning as the construction of meaning, it becomes clearer and clearer that the students must also be part of the "our" in "our work."

One of the great social tragedies of our time is the extent to which inner cities are viewed as wholly separate from their surrounding suburbs, especially by the suburbanites. Indeed, most suburbanites became suburbanites to escape central cities. Yet, it is clear that the problems of urban education will inevitably spill over into the surrounding suburbs. In western New York, we have very gingerly approached the issue of helping people to see how interdependent the education systems are. One of the more interesting projects has been a pairing of several social studies classes from the suburbs with similar classes from the central city. They visited each other's classes and engaged in discussions about their respective schools and environments. They even attended a play and concert together as a way of coming to understand each other. "Our work" must include such cross-district collaborations.

Finally, building on the kinds of collaborations with school people outlined above in discussing our work in the university, it is important for school faculty and administrators to see themselves as part of a continuum of professional development processes. Preservice education will likely remain largely the responsibility of higher education, but we need the help of the schools (Darling-Hammond, 1994; Petrie, 1995b). For their part, schools cannot continue to assume that newly minted teachers are automatically fully competent to take over their own classrooms. Mentor teachers and other continuing professional development activities will be needed, with higher education and other staff development resources playing adjunct roles. Schools themselves, in collaboration with others, must come to see continuing education of their staff as a major part of our joint work.

What Is "Our Work"?

Any number of commentators have made it clear that education is essentially a value-laden enterprise (Cuban, 1992; Nyberg & Egan, 1981; Peters, 1967; Shujaa, 1994). This leaves open the question of what or whose values, and that is not a question that I intend to address in this chapter. Suffice it to say that, following Dewey (1944/1966; see also Petrie, 1971), I believe that agreement on values can, for the most part, be decided through careful reasoning and the application of the scientific method. In short, it is not just a matter of taste, despite the numerous examples of value conflicts where the evidence is not yet as clear as it might be.

For my purposes, I will simply assert that the ultimate guiding value for our work in education must be the learning of children. This will encompass those who believe that what children should learn is primarily revealed in some religious text as well as those who believe that children should learn mathematics and science so as to be able to compete in an information age. The focus in either case is on children's learning.

If we focus primarily on children's learning, then we can "backward map" onto the kinds of things others in the educational professions should be doing. Teachers must know the things that children should learn, how these are determined, and who determines them. They must know how to present those things in ways that lead to children learning them. They must understand child development and the nature of learning and teaching. As professionals they need to appreciate the sociopolitical context in which they work as well as the environments that shape their students' lives.

Administrators/leaders need to know much the same things as do teachers, with more emphasis on the organizational, social, and political-economic context of schooling. They must also have clearly in mind the end of education as the learning of all children and should try to keep everyone focused on that goal. They must have a grasp of group processes and be problem solvers. One of their highest values should be to facilitate others—primarily teachers and students—in achieving their goals.

Pupil personnel professionals such as counselors, psychologists, special education teachers, specialists in reading, and the like must see their work as contributing to student learning. For example, the school psychologist must consider it her job to assist student learning, not simply to provide some sort of independent psychological assessment of the student. Similarly, the school counselor's work as part of the educational process is not that of a private practitioner helping with the overall development of the students as persons, but one of helping students learn.

Taking another step in the backward mapping, those of us who prepare educational professionals—from teachers and administrators to counselors and psychologists—need to construct our curricula and preparation programs so that the professionals we prepare will have the values, capacities, and dispositions they need to enhance the learning of all students. In a way, this would not be denied by any university professor. Yet we have administrator preparation programs that contain virtually no reference to curricular matters. We have teacher education programs with little, if any, focus on the socioeconomic environments that affect the learning of students. We have counselor education courses of study in which the students never interact with teachers or administrators.

And, like the embarrassed silence when I asked my faculty what they meant by "school" and what role they thought the professionals they prepared played in that institution, there is virtually total silence in the different programs about other professionals. If education is truly the joint work of a wide variety of educational professionals, the "glue" that holds it together is invisible to all of them and the results have little, if any, relationship to anyone's explicit goals.

Achieving Shared Values

Even assuming that educational professionals share the overall value of promoting student learning for all children, that is far too abstract an ideal by itself to bring a variety of educational professionals, to say nothing of parents and students, together into a common work agenda. Each of these constituencies—indeed, each individual participant in the process—has any number of additional values that are also in play and that can lead to many conflicts.

To cite just one example, most teachers value their professional expertise and do not relish being told what to do by either administrators or parents.

Administrators, however, value an organization that achieves results; occasionally, they have to deal with teachers who are not pulling their weight.

Parents value their roles as the primary educators of their children and are often loathe to turn over that education to a stranger, especially one who may not value the same things as the parent does.

Can any progress be made toward finding shared values? Without being able to outline any kind of recipe, I do want to make two observations that may help. First, people operate under a hierarchy of values, and conflict at a lower level may be resolvable at a higher level where agreement can be found. Second, there are ways to explore one's own and others' value hierarchies to begin to determine where there are conflicts and where there may be unsuspected levels of agreement. I will sketch how each of these things is possible.

First, the existence of value hierarchies is easy to demonstrate. To take just one simple example, I value working at my job. In order to do that, I have come to take a certain route to work every morning. So, one of my lower-order goals in the morning is to travel down Sheridan to Ayer and over to Maple and on to the entrance to the university. However, if Ayer is blocked, I don't have any trouble at all continuing on Sheridan to Youngs, thereby changing my lower-order goal of traveling a certain route in order to achieve my higher-order goal of getting to work. Indeed, this kind of adaptability of all human beings is so common we seldom remark about it except in those rare cases where someone is absolutely obsessive about something we believe to be silly. Why don't they just adapt?

But my goal of working at my job is itself subservient to other higher-order goals. One of the higher-order values served by my job is making enough money to enjoy a reasonably comfortable life. Should my job disappear, I would surely look for another one. The situation gets more complicated here, however, because not only does my job bring in money, it also involves other things that I value—intellectual challenge, work with interesting people, sharing my knowledge, and so on. Were I forced to try to find another job out of economic necessity, I would surely try to look for one that also allowed me to pursue being the kind of person I want to be.

The same mechanism of changing lower-order goals in order to achieve higher-order goals in an uncertain and changing world is at work in dealing with conflict with others. If one can move to a higher-level goal, the conflict often disappears. An example comes from our discussions regarding the number of different degree programs offered by the Graduate School of Education. For a number of reasons, every different teaching specialization is represented by a different degree. This situation makes it difficult to change curricula without gaining approval of all sorts of state agencies. On the other hand, if we had only a few degrees with different concentrations, changing the concentrations would be much simpler.

When I raised this possibility with the faculty, there was significant opposition to giving up any of the degrees. As we discussed the situation further, it became apparent that the faculty were worried that a student with a degree in education with a concentration in English education might not be as employable as would one with a degree in English education. Indeed, they were worried in the case of master's students that the students might not be certifiable.

When I found out that the higher-order goal was to provide employability for the students rather than any inherent attachment to individualized degrees, I was able to provide evidence of other institutions in New York and elsewhere in the country whose degrees were much less specifically labeled than ours. The students in those programs were able to obtain positions, so the faculty could retain their higher-order goal of helping their students get jobs while also making curriculum changes more easily.

This example also illustrates the general procedure one needs to use to determine what someone's values really are and where they reside in the person's values hierarchy. If someone values something, he or she will resist those situations that get in the way of the realization of the values. Hence, the faculty resisted my early attempts to simplify our degree structures. However, the lower-order value of specialized degrees was recognized as being in the service of the higher-order value of helping students obtain jobs. Once the value of helping students obtain jobs is seen as realizable without specialized degrees, then changing to a more generalized degree structure may not be resisted after all.

This procedure may sound like common sense in that one simply talks to people to find ways in which they can realize their values in their everyday lives. However, it is a stronger procedure than just asking people what they want. In principle, we can find out the highest-order values people have even if they themselves do not always know what those values are. We change the environments in various ways, usually imaginatively through conversations exploring alternatives, and see what people wish to hold onto most strongly. Those are likely to be the highest-order and most strongly held values.

This procedure gives us a handle on how we might begin to focus on "our work" together. We can ask ourselves and our would-be collaborators what we are really after. Insofar as we share the higher-order value of improving children's learning, then it is at least in principle possible for us to see how university faculty of various stripes can continue to be recognized scholars in their fields, effective teachers, and helpful staff developers. As the university is changing in response to external pressures, it becomes easier for faculty to see that field-based research and professional activities can both further the cause of children's learning as well as their own academic reputations and rewards. Similarly, school people can continue to be good teachers, make a decent living, and see themselves as valued collaborators in school reform.

In the end, it is absolutely essential that an appropriate balance be struck between "my work" and "our work." Both of these typically involve essential values for educators—both university and school faculty. Through a careful exploration of the values structures of the would-be collaborators it will in many instances be possible to see "my work" as an essential part of "our work."

There is, however, no guarantee that this will happen. It is possible that even the most detailed elaboration of the participants' value structures will leave them in conflict at some level. A faculty member in a professional school of education may be simply unable to see her or his academic work as connected to education or schooling as opposed to contributing to the basic theories of a discipline. Such a faculty member would do better in a disciplinary-oriented department. A school teacher may be unable to view him- or herself as a coach or facilitator of the construction of students' learning and, hence, may always have to be the "sage on the stage."

The point, however, is that if we are to have any chance at all of moving from "my work" to "our work," we will have to explore the value structures of the participants and determine the extent to which they can be made compatible with each other. Note, too, that this is not simply another version of the often-heard admonition that you have to get everyone's "buy-in." You do, indeed, need buy-in, but people will buy in only if they see the enterprise as furthering their own deep-seated values. This also implies that talk of changing reward structures to obtain buy-in is a bit too superficial. Rewards are rewards only if people find them to be such. For example, we all respond somewhat to monetary rewards, but only somewhat, and different people respond to different degrees.

Even such motivators as fear for our lives have limits, as indicated by the old Jack Benny story. Jack Benny is accosted by an armed robber who says, "Your money or your life!" Benny says nothing. The robber says, "Didn't you hear me? I said, your money or your life!" Benny responds, "I'm thinking. I'm thinking." The story is funny precisely because it is not entirely out of the realm of possibility that, for Benny, money is more important than his life. Or think of classical martyrs. Clearly there were values for them that were more important than their lives.

In the final analysis, then, "our work" must come from and be a part of "my work." We cannot impose "our work." However, we also need not rest content with simply allowing ourselves to pursue our individual work. We can and must explore the intersections.

Challenges and Necessary Reformulations

What does this view of the highly contextualized nature of "our work" have to say with respect to some of the common wisdom found in the school reform rhetoric? Do we have a "knowledge base" waiting to be applied to school reform? Can we generalize results from the lighthouse projects that do seem to work? What about "going to scale" with reforms that work? What is the nature of accountability for educational reform?

As the social sciences are beginning to realize from a number of perspectives (Petrie, 1995a), the dream of finding general laws of learning or teaching or schooling that constitute a knowledge base is almost surely a vain hope. For a variety of reasons, from the complexity of human behavior to the epistemology of psychological explanation, human action is constantly varying in detail in order to achieve consistent ends. Recall my example of finding different paths to my office. Think about the varying ways in which good teachers will respond to different scenarios in their classrooms, no two of which will be similar. They will vary their techniques considerably, and yet they are often successful in helping their students to learn.

Rather than talk about a knowledge base that conjures up images of general laws waiting to be applied in every new situation, the ideas of "our work" sketched in this chapter suggest a much more contextualized approach. "Our work" is to jointly bring what knowledge and skill we have to the task of helping John and Suzy and Keisha and Muhammed and Carlos learn what they need to know. Others may be able to learn from our efforts, but that learning will be more in the nature of the ways in which we learn from reading literature or case studies than from how we might learn general laws to apply to new situations. Indeed, this kind of approach is much more compatible with emerging conceptions of, for example, teacher research (Cochran-Smith & Lytle, 1990; Petrie, 1995a; see also Chapter 5).

In this sense, the concept of a knowledge base for education is highly misleading. Indeed, such a notion reinforces the idea that teaching is an applied, technical activity that can simply take general laws and apply them to concrete cases. Although there are technical, applied aspects to teaching, it is not fundamentally an applied activity in the Aristotelian sense of answering the question, "How do I do this?" Rather, it is aimed at answering the practical question, "What ought I to do, here and now, in this situation, with these students?" Education is, ineluctably, value laden and context bound.

It is because education is both a value-laden as well as a context-sensitive activity that "our work" in one place may be different than "our work" in another place. This fact may help explain why results from an educational experiment in one place so seldom generalize to another place. It would, of course, be nice if we simply could replicate educational successes, in cookie-cutter fashion. And it may be that there are some educational "technologies" (Pogrow, 1996) that can and should be learned by a wide variety of practitioners. However, in the end, the balance between my work and our work must be struck in each context.

This value-laden and context-sensitive feature of education casts serious doubt upon the possibility of "going to scale" with educational reforms that seem to work. What we seem to be learning from current successes is that it is not "programs" in the classical sense that can be replicated on a larger scale. Rather, what we need to bring to scale are the kinds of policy and financial supports that will encourage local cadres of teachers, administrators, parents, professors, and students to do the work in thousands of different contexts and situations. This approach, however, is not "the American way." It places fundamental reliance on people and their professional judgments rather than on things and technologies. It invests in knowledge and competence (Darling-Hammond, 1989) rather than in externally devised programs. It will be difficult to sell to those who want quick fixes.

It might be argued that the "value-ladenness" and context specificity that I have been describing is simply a smoke screen for educators wanting to avoid real accountability. It is saying, "Trust us, and, not only that, but give us the resources to do whatever we want." Such an objection might carry some weight if we remain with "my work" which is not subject to any external negotiations. However, if we have truly moved from "my work" to "our work," we will have reached a broad agreement among the various constituencies in education on what that joint, collaborative work is. That, in turn, will allow us to appeal to the kind of accountability that professionals have in pursuing the agreed-upon goals of their profession. It is an accountability that arises from the values that have come to inform "our work."

The politicians and the public will be able to "trust *us*" precisely because we will jointly have been engaged in the dialogue and debate necessary to define what "our work" as educators means in our society. We will have negotiated a new social contract with the larger society that supports us, and a part of that contract will concern the forms of accountability that we have jointly undertaken. It will be neither an accountability imposed from above, nor a license for educators to do what they will with no constraints whatsoever. It will be "our work" of educating the next generations.

References

Boyer, E. L. (1990). *Scholarship reconsidered: Priorities of the professoriate*. Princeton, NJ: Carnegie Foundation for the Advancement of Teaching.

Clifford, G. J., & Guthrie, J. W. (1988). *Ed school: A brief for professional education.* Chicago: University of Chicago Press.

Cochran-Smith, M., & Lytle, S. L. (1990). Research on teaching and teacher research: The issues that divide. *Educational Researcher, 19*(2), 2-11.

Cornbleth, C., & Ellsworth, J. (1994). Clinical faculty in teacher education: Roles and Relationships. *American Educational Research Journal, 31*(1), 49-70.

Cuban, L. (1992). Managing dilemmas while building professional communities. *Educational Researcher, 21*(1), 4-11.

Darling-Hammond, L. (1989). Accountability for professional practice. *Teachers College Record, 91*(1), 59-80.

Darling-Hammond, L. (Ed.). (1994). *Professional development schools: Schools for developing a profession.* New York: Teachers College Press.

Dewey, J. (1960). *The quest for certainty: A study of the relation of knowledge and action.* New York: Putnam. (Original work published 1929)

Dewey, J. (1966). *Democracy and education: An introduction to the philosophy of education.* New York: Free Press. (Original work published 1944)

Ellsworth, J., & Albers, C. M. (1995). Tradition and authority in teacher education reform. In H. Petrie (Ed.), *Professionalization, partnership, and power: Building professional development schools* (pp.159-176). Albany: State University of New York Press.

Holmes Group. (1986). *Tomorrow's teachers: A report of the Holmes Group.* East Lansing, MI: Author.

Holmes Group. (1990). *Tomorrow's schools: A report of the Holmes Group.* East Lansing, MI: Author.

Holmes Group. (1995). *Tomorrow's schools of education: A report of the Holmes Group.* East Lansing, MI: Author.

Jencks, C., & Riesman, D. (1969). *The academic revolution.* Garden City, NY: Anchor Books.

Judge, H. G. (1982). *American graduate schools of education: A view from abroad: A report to the Ford Foundation.* New York: The Ford Foundation.

Knapp, M. S., Barnard, K., Brandon, R. N., Gehrke, N. J., Smith, A. J., & Teather, E. C. (1993). University-based preparation for collaborative interprofessional practice. In L. Adler & S. Gardner (Eds.), *The politics of linking schools and social services. The 1993 Yearbook of the Politics of Education Association,* pp. 137-151.

Nyberg, D., & Egan, K. (1981). *The erosion of education: Socialization and the schools.* New York: Teachers College, Columbia University.

Peters, R. S. (Ed.). (1967). *The concept of education*. London: Routledge & Kegan Paul.

Petrie, H. G. (1971, Winter). Practical reasoning: Some examples. *Philosophy and Rhetoric, 4,* 29-41.

Petrie, H. G. (1992). "I can do that!": A case study of a teaching development program. In S. Hills (Ed.), *The history and philosophy of science in science education, Vol. II* (pp. 603-613). Kingston, Ontario: Queen's University.

Petrie, H. G. (1995a). A new paradigm for practical research. In H. Petrie (Ed.), *Professionalization, partnership, and power: Building professional development schools* (pp. 285-302). Albany: State University of New York Press.

Petrie, H. G. (Ed.). (1995b). *Professionalization, partnership, and power: Building professional development schools*. Albany: State University of New York Press.

Pogrow, S. (1996). Reforming the wannabe reformers. *Phi Delta Kappan, 77,* 656-663.

Shujaa, M. J. (Ed.). (1994). *Too much schooling, too little education: A paradox of black life in white societies*. Trenton, NJ: Africa World Press.

3

Beyond Teaching:
Learning to Lead
Through Action Research

Catherine Emihovich

Historically, schools have played a conservative role of maintaining the status quo in preparing students to enter a society whose parameters were relatively stable. This is no longer the situation. Schools today are undergoing profound changes in how the educational system is administered, as old models of centralized authority derived from a state bureaucracy are replaced by site-based management models and shared decision making. These changes in turn require new kinds of behaviors from the professionals who staff the schools, particularly among the teachers who spend the most time with students and exert the greatest influence over their school careers. Some of the skills that will be needed are the ability to create curriculum frameworks that incorporate new forms of knowledge, collaborate with peers on shared concerns related to students' progress, assume leadership roles on school improvement councils, and develop an authoritative voice about the production of new scholarship related to teaching and learning issues.

Unfortunately, because the "structure of teaching develops a kind of radical individualism, teachers are typically conservative agents of continuity, rather than dynamic agents of change" (Ayers, 1992, p. 19). Another contributing factor as to why teachers have not played a strong role in educational reform efforts is due to the marginalization of teachers' voices

AUTHOR'S NOTE: I would like to thank Frances Kochan for her invaluable insight and assistance in helping me understand how a model of action research could be applied to the preparation of new teachers.

concerning their beliefs and practices. One reason is that they deal with children, historically a low-status occupation, and one further complicated by the fact that they are expected to rectify all of today's youths' social problems in the absence of traditional societal supports (Spencer, 1996). In the case of teachers who held onto the ideals they had in college of making a difference in children's lives, too often these teachers have found themselves working in a school environment that is autocratic, alienating, and deadening to their spirits and those of the students.

If schools are to become "learning communities," to use Ayers's (1992) apt phrase, teachers clearly need to develop a new vision of their role and to enact new behaviors that embody this role. At the same time, the ways in which new and experienced teachers acquire the knowledge and skills to become effective teachers will also need to change. The old model of staff development for inservice credit where teachers sit through endless lectures from outside "experts" will need to be replaced by models that empower teachers to take action based on critical reflections about key components of the teaching/learning process. Teacher education programs will also need to change to incorporate the rich body of knowledge that has accumulated on how to teach for understanding (Brown, 1994), instead of just delivering content; how to scaffold learning to meet the needs of diverse learners (Palincsar, 1986), instead of assuming that all learners are the same; how to develop curriculum frameworks that draw upon expert subject knowledge (Shulman, 1987), instead of relying on watered-down content; and, finally, how to assess authentic learning that is complex and multidimensional in its outcomes (Darling-Hammond, Ancess, & Falk, 1995), instead of relying upon measures that use predetermined answers to multiple-choice questions.

How do we get these new kinds of teachers? In her 1996 AERA Presidential Address, Linda Darling-Hammond suggested that one way is to engage teachers in the inquiry process where they investigate aspects of their practice and become observers and documenters of children's learning. As Darling-Hammond (1996) noted,

> Teacher engagement in research helps create a clientele for profession-wide knowledge while it also builds teachers' personal knowledge of students and learning in ways that are often transformatory for teaching. (p. 12)

The concept of engaging practitioners in research within their settings that is directly connected with their practice is not new; this concept, known as action research, originated from the work of Kurt Lewin in the 1940s and became prominent in education in the 1970s through the work of Lawrence Stenhouse and his colleagues in Great Britain and Australia (Elliott, 1990; Rudduck & Hopkins, 1985). Increasingly, calls for action research in American schools have proliferated in the last decade (Kincheloe, 1991; Noffke & Stevenson, 1994). Action research appears to be an ideal model because of its emphasis on critical self-reflection of one's behaviors and its orientation to solving immediate and practical problems. More important for education, it can also incorporate an explicitly activist stance whereby teachers are asked not only to reflect on their practice and take specific actions but also to use these actions to pursue social justice and equity in learning. This model of action research draws upon the work of Kemmis and McTaggart (1988), who noted,

> Action research is a form of collective self-reflective inquiry undertaken by participants in a social situation in order to improve the rationality and justice of their own social practices, as well as their understanding of these practices and the situations in which these practices are carried out. (p. 5)

In this chapter, I discuss the implications of organizing a teacher education program around an action research framework. To do so, I draw upon the experience and knowledge gained from implementing this model in the context of preparing teachers at a large public state university. Asking teachers to consider themselves as teacher-researchers entails asking them to build upon and extend behaviors that are already familiar to good teachers, but now with the proviso of having them articulate more clearly and defensibly the reasons for choosing specific practices in the classroom. And once they have reflected on the reasons for their choices, they are in a better position to take action in changing their practice, and then assessing the impact of this change. By engaging in inquiry, teachers, members of a profession in the public school sector historically dominated by women, can reclaim their right to speak about their profession on their own terms. As Giroux (1988) noted,

> Teachers also need to be conscious of their own voices so that they can understand how their own values and experiences work to produce, legitimate, and structure how they respond to the various voices that make up their classroom. (p. 9)

Meaningful educational change is neither easy nor painless. Moving a university-based teacher education program in a new direction that emphasizes strengthening the teacher's voice through engagement in an action-oriented inquiry process, and fostering collaborative partnerships with local school districts, becomes more difficult when districts have become accustomed to the university setting the standards while grumbling about its inability to change. I will candidly not only present the positive aspects of our program but also discuss some of the problems and concerns that arise when a new program is introduced that contradicts people's expectations of what teachers are supposed to do. I will close by suggesting that changes in how teachers are prepared will not lead to the desired outcomes in the classroom unless the ways in which administrators are prepared change as well.

Making Collaboration Work

Without question, the need for closer collaboration between school districts and university professional education programs in order to facilitate meaningful educational change is widely acknowledged to be greater than ever (Fullan, 1991; Lieberman, 1990). Yet what is often missing in the professional literature is a detailed description of how these collaborative efforts are launched, along with a candid portrayal of missed opportunities and miscommunications, as well as the successes such efforts can engender. In BRIET's case, a strong core of programmatic elements for developing closer relationships with schools that would enhance teachers' professional development was already in place. These elements included the use of clinical faculty for teaching methods classes, the Associated Schools program, and the concept of the BRIET liaison and on-site field teams.[1] The challenge facing the BRIET staff was how to incorporate new directions in teacher education, particularly the need to develop inquiry-oriented teachers who not only engaged in critical reflections of their practice but took action to change it when warranted. And more important, an even greater challenge was how to connect this shift with the needs of school districts to have a well-prepared staff who could help them meet in turn the new standards for teaching and learning being established at state and national levels. In the next three sections, I discuss the processes involved in embedding an action research model within BRIET over a 3-year period, and how I believe it contributes to students' increased understanding of teaching as well as their development of leadership capabilities.

"Ready, Fire, Aim!": First-Year Implementation

In the fall of 1994, I was hired as the new director of BRIET, and one of my goals was to implement an action research model that I had developed while working at another public state university in Florida. While there, my involvement in the teacher education program was based on teaching an undergraduate educational psychology course that was required for all students in the program. Working closely with the director of the laboratory school in Florida that the university maintained on its premises, I recruited 20 teachers who indicated they were interested in the idea of becoming teacher researchers by using action research methods in their classroom. Each teacher was given a team of undergraduate students from my class to help them observe and record data relevant to their classroom practices. The teacher and students worked as a team in selecting and researching the questions being addressed. At the end of the semester, the students wrote up the action research results, which provided the teacher with a valuable resource that enabled them to acquire a more distanced perspective on the problem being addressed. This approach enabled the classroom teacher to view his or her concerns more critically, while also giving the undergraduate students a unique opportunity to view classroom behaviors firsthand and to discuss their meaning with an experienced teacher.

Using this model as a template, in the fall of 1994 a seminar was held with all cooperating teachers in BRIET's Associated Schools. They were informed that BRIET would now incorporate tenets of action research in the program and that the preservice teachers would be expected to carry out a small action research project during their student teaching experience. Several teachers had heard of action research through professional development workshops and were eager to work with a student teacher in focusing on a question to explore jointly. Other teachers who were less familiar with this model agreed to have the student pursue a question without their involvement. The students were introduced to action research through small group seminars held to discuss aspects of the teaching process.[2] Although it would be fair to say that most of the cooperating teachers and preservice teachers had no deep understanding of the action research process based on their limited exposure to it, they did their best to focus on examining some aspect of practice in the classroom. Several projects turned out surprisingly well, and many of the teachers who were initially resistant to the idea became enthusiastic converts to using action research. They signed up to have a student teacher the next year who would be doing the same thing.

Fullan (1991) has spoken of educational change as a process that often needs a jump start beyond the endless rounds of talk about change; hence, his use of the phrase, "ready, fire, aim." In this case the aim was clear on BRIET's part, but it was not necessarily shared by the administrators and cooperating teachers. To allay their concerns, and to develop a better sense of schools' needs in terms of formulating action research questions, informational seminars were held with administrators, teachers, parents, and community members in five different school districts during the spring 1995 semester. We also held an orientation session to which all the principals and BRIET liaisons in our Associated Schools were invited in order to give them more detailed information about the new model. In retrospect, it would have been more useful to have begun implementation of this new model with both processes to give district administrators and teachers an opportunity to express their concerns about how new teachers were prepared. It is a rare case when school districts are invited to give feedback prior to programmatic changes at the university level, even when those changes directly affect the school's operation and its personnel. In bringing this model to BRIET from another university, I had overlooked the fact that my close relationship with the teachers and the director of the laboratory school, which had been built through several years work with the school, had facilitated the preservice students' entry into the classrooms. Although some of the projects had been successful, people's normal resistance to change was strengthened by being asked to participate in a program whose goals and aims were not clearly understood or shared. Fullan (1991) quoted Marris to the effect that any innovation "cannot be assimilated until its *meaning* is shared (p. 31; emphasis in original).

One aspect that obviously needed to change based on the preservice and cooperating teachers' comments during the evaluation process was that the action research project had to occur earlier in the program. Although the preservice students felt the experience had been beneficial, they also felt that student teaching was not the best time to be doing it because they were stressed out trying simultaneously to master other aspects of teaching such as lesson planning and classroom management. The cooperating teachers also stated they would have liked more information on how to do action research, either as part of inservice staff development meetings or in workshops.

Creating Shared Dialogues: Second-Year Implementation

As a result of holding the informational sessions with the school districts in the spring, 26 teachers from two school districts (one urban, one suburban) signed up for an action research workshop taught in the fall 1995 semester to become more proficient in action research techniques. At the same time, all teachers agreed to take on a preservice student who would be assigned to their classes to assist them in conducting their project. In addition, five teachers (two math, two English from two high schools, and one middle school social studies teacher) agreed to have the same student continue on in their class for the student's first student teaching placement.[3] The preservice students were enrolled in the undergraduate section of the required educational psychology class, and the major change was that now they would do their action research project in the fall (except for the five students), and then do their student teaching in the spring, albeit at a different school. The remaining BRIET students who were enrolled in the graduate section of the same class (about two thirds of the students) were no longer required to do an action research project, because we had learned that it was too difficult for them to manage it during the student teaching phase, and no arrangements had been made to have them spend extended time in a school during the fall semester. These students, however, continued to observe in various schools in the fall as part of their field experience class. The decision to limit participation only to the undergraduate students was based on the fact that this was a pilot project designed to implement a new phase in the BRIET program that had the following goals:

1. Facilitate a long-term placement in one school so that the student teacher would have time to learn more about the school culture and organizational structure
2. Develop closer relationships with the students
3. Establish a more collegial relationship with an experienced teacher who would become a mentor and not just a cooperating teacher offering up a classroom in which to practice his or her teaching skills

If it proved successful, we decided we would direct our attention to actively recruiting teachers during the spring and summer who would be willing to accept a student in the fall for the purpose of conducting an action research project, and then serve as the student's first placement teacher in the spring. Ideally, students would then have almost 6 months' experience in the same school, which, given the current constraints of our program, was the closest approximation to an internship that we could develop.

With one exception, the students' experience in the classes where they were able to do both an action research project and remain in the same school for student teaching was highly successful. The action research process proved to be an excellent vehicle for allowing the preservice student to ask questions about aspects of teaching practices that puzzled them, and to learn more about the students' lives and their interests in school. This comment by one young woman is typical of students' reactions:

It built in reflection and I found myself reflecting more on teaching. The research had nothing to do with me; it was asking the students what they thought. What they say shapes what they know. . . . There is a different type of conversation going on in my head. The kids were sincere and I learned from them. This project was different from the others; it had a life, it had a "real story" behind it.

For their part, the cooperating teachers felt they had a better opportunity to learn more about the student teacher's strengths and weaknesses in their readiness to teach, and they were able to develop a more collegial mentor relationship. The teachers mentioned on their evaluation form that they felt having a student observe their practice "renewed their enthusiasm" and forced them to "do more critical thinking and articulate their ideas about teaching."

Our experience during this year encouraged us to believe that we were on the right track in having students engage in action research as a way of reflecting on teaching. At the same time, we realized that the curriculum needed to be restructured to ensure that students were receiving a consistent message across their professional courses. We were also concerned about gaps in the curriculum that needed to be addressed, such as helping teachers incorporate new technologies in learning; preparing them to handle culturally and linguistically diverse students, as well as students with special needs; and making them aware of the new trend in developing integrated services on-site for at-risk students. One of our operating constraints was that we did not have the luxury of simply adding new courses to accommodate these needs; instead, we had to find a way to integrate this information into the existing curriculum, and to do so without treading on the toes of faculty who had taught these courses for many years.

Restructuring Curriculum: Third-Year Implementation

During the spring and summer of 1996, several significant events occurred that enabled us to move toward our goal of expanding the extended placement model to include all students enrolled in the program. A curriculum retreat was planned and well attended by several GSE faculty involved in teacher education as well as school personnel who were actively involved in BRIET activities. This retreat enabled us to inform people about new directions the program was taking, as well as hear about concerns that practitioners wanted us to address in the curriculum. This retreat was followed by a 2-day meeting in the summer attended by GSE teaching faculty, clinical faculty, and BRIET staff to begin developing an integrated curriculum for all

BRIET courses. For the first time, a master schedule was created that listed all the topics covered week by week in all the courses. This schedule was created in response to BRIET students' complaints that there was too little coordination and consistency across courses and that they were often confused by the conflicting messages they received about the importance of particular topics from different instructors. This kind of collaborative curriculum building, which is becoming more common in public schools, is still rarely seen in colleges of education, where professors are given complete autonomy to structure their courses as they wish, regardless of whether or not they conform to the demands of the field.

Despite the progress made in attracting some of the regular faculty to work on an integrated curriculum model, much work remains to be done. One of BRIET's future goals is to develop a cohort group model similar to the one described in Chapter 4 for students enrolled in an experimental educational administration program. In this model, students do not take specific courses but rather are involved in a cumulative set of experiences and activities that provide them with the skills and background information expected of professionals in the field. To make this happen for teacher education students, a very well thought out, collaborative working relationship would need to be developed among the GSE faculty, BRIET staff, and faculty from one or more schools that could be described as professional development schools. A relationship at this level of cooperation does not yet exist. Its formation depends upon (a) shedding traditional expectations of what college faculty are rewarded for doing; (b) professional staff development for classroom teachers that is more innovative than just listening to outside experts, and (c) most important, a shared understanding that this kind of model is the one needed to produce teachers who are capable of dealing with educational and organizational change that is unprecedented in scope.

Building Connections: The Goals 2000 Project

At the same time that BRIET was undergoing a restructuring of its curriculum, other initiatives were pursued to expand collaborative linkages with school districts not currently affiliated with the BRIET program. One of these initiatives served to connect BRIET more closely to educational leadership preparation. During the spring 1996 semester, three GSE faculty (Stephen Jacobson, Robert Stevenson, and myself) cowrote and received a Goals 2000 grant in collaboration with the Niagara Falls School District, represented by the director of staff development, Catherine Battaglia. The purpose of the grant was to embed the tenets of action research within the district's Professional Growth Plan. Three teams were recruited: a team of science teachers from one high school, a team that was developing an integrated curriculum for ninth graders at another high school, and an interdisciplinary team from a middle school. Each team also included one administrator, because all four of us believed strongly that changes in teachers' practice must be accompanied by corresponding changes in organizational practices at the building level if these changes are to be successful. During the spring, the teams attended workshops about action research and planned and conducted small projects within their schools. They were assisted in their endeavors by undergraduate students who were enrolled in a pre-BRIET class, one where students discussed current educational issues and observed schools in order to decide whether they were interested in teaching as a career. The three science teachers also agreed to take on a BRIET student for the extended placement model in the fall 1996 semester.

This project differed from our previous work with teachers in conducting action research. Each school sent a group of teachers and administrators that ostensibly worked as a team in identifying a common concern that lent itself to the teams' taking action in resolving it. Although in practice not all the teams worked as smoothly as we had hoped, we learned that more attention needs to paid to helping educators work cooperatively if they are to implement this concept at the classroom level. We realized at the end that the process of developing facilitative leadership skills within the groups was as important as teaching them about the action research process itself.

This experience also affirmed the importance of including an administrator on the team and highlighted the need for providing them with opportunities to reflect upon the issue of how they might restructure their school to use more effectively a cadre of teachers who were empowered through action research to take on more leadership roles within the school. Here again we also experienced clashes with the principals' traditional notions of who was responsible for leadership within a school setting, because we observed at times within the groups' discussion that the principals reverted back to a pattern of taking charge of the discussion and expecting the teachers to follow their lead. Several of the teachers seemed content to sit back and let the principal take charge, even though they were beginning to question some long-standing traditional practices within their school. This situation was similar to the one described by Clift, Veal, Johnson, and Holland (1990), who noted in their action research project the importance of having the principal involved in creating a professional culture of learning. However, as they pointed out, this created tensions within the group because "the teachers' natural inclination is to look to the principal as a superordinate; the principal's

natural inclination is to lead through organizing action" (p. 57). If collaborative action research is to succeed, teachers must learn to feel comfortable in
a leadership role and see themselves as having a vested interest in what occurs
within the whole school, instead of only being focused on students' behavior
within the classroom.

Unfinished Business: Sustaining Collaboration

What worked? Despite a rocky beginning in the first year, the efforts to
reach out to the districts paid off in terms of increasing support for the goal of
preparing a more professionally oriented teacher, one who not only reflected
on aspects of his or her practice but, through specific actions, was able to
identify the ways in which it could be improved. Despite the positive effects
of these initial collaborative efforts, however, vexing problems in the differ-
ential status and power between faculty in public schools and universities still
need to be resolved (Campbell, 1988; Cochran-Smith & Lytle, 1990). The
shift to a more professional orientation in the preparation of new teachers
raises a number of questions about issues such as who controls knowledge
production in education, how much voice should practitioners (who quite
often hold advanced degrees equivalent to their university counterparts)
have in establishing the next directions in a professional education program,
and the degree to which change can occur through a consensual process.
As the BRIET staff works closely with schools to continue a dialogue on how
best to prepare teachers, all of us need to remain mindful of Elliott's (1993)
assertion that "the dialogue and debate with others always will be from a limited and partial perspective" (p. 204). From our "limited and partial perspective" as university faculty, we recognize that we still have unfinished business
that must be resolved if school/university collaborations are to succeed.

Teachers as Leaders of Change

One school of thought holds that action research can be perceived as a
means by which teachers take on a more activist role in advocating change to
ensure that concerns related to social justice and equity are addressed even
though this stance may bring them into conflict with the more "objective" stance
expected from a professional (Zeichner, 1991). Although not all of the people
who teach courses for BRIET students necessarily espouse the idea that all
action research projects must lead to this end, collectively we do recognize
the dilemma faced by new, idealistic teachers who sincerely want the results
of their actions to change conditions they feel work to students' disadvantages.

A consistent message suggested to preservice and inservice teachers is that they be clear about the reasons for pursuing a particular course of action and that they act upon their convictions in asking hard questions about the educational process. An issue that has already surfaced among BRIET students in my graduate educational psychology class is what they should do when school officials react negatively to actions taken in the classroom that challenge conventional routines. A good example is the case of a history teacher who wants to present a more controversial view of history (e.g., the conquest of the West as told from the Native American point of view) but who finds that other colleagues and some parents are unsympathetic to this action. If teachers are truly to become leaders and masters of their profession, they should be free to investigate problematic issues within the school or raise concerns about curriculum materials that fail to keep students motivated. Questions of equity and social justice are precisely the ones that idealistic children and adolescents want most to discuss, and quite often they are the ones that capture students' attention and increase their motivation to attend class.[4] When teachers believe they are not free to engage in actions that in their professional judgment meet students' needs, they are often forced into a defensive teaching mode that benefits no one (McNeil, 1989) and serves to drive some of the most talented and creative candidates away from teaching.

The role of professional development schools in promoting a culture in which issues of social justice and equity are linked to teaching and learning is one that has received scant attention in most school/university collaborative partnerships. According to an extensive review (Valli, Cooper, & Frankes, 1997), "professional development in the majority of partnerships revolves around the instrumental and technical concerns of teaching" (p. 274). The authors also note,

> While the PDS cannot serve as a panacea for the severe inequalities that characterize life for many in this society, a more deliberate link between the mission of the PDS as an instrument of political and social reform and the daily work of educators may support the invention of a truly new organization. (Valli, Cooper, & Frankes, 1997, p. 293)

The issue of whether action research should be explicitly oriented around an agenda of social change is one we have yet to resolve in conversations with our professional partners. The issue is further complicated by a topic unmentioned in the professional literature—a situation where students (and/or their teachers) choose to do action research on issues that conflict with the philosophical stance of the teacher education program. A case in point might be the decision of staff within a school to agree that tracking best serves the interests of the school and community in preparing students for different careers, and the action research project was organized around this philosophy. At the same time, the preservice student might be learning about research that challenges the efficacy of tracking and underscores its detrimental effects on student achievement, especially in terms of race and class differences (Oakes, 1985). In this case, the student teacher would face a serious dilemma in being asked to work on a project that may conflict with beliefs he or she is acquiring at the university. This case also highlights the dichotomy between the university faculty's claim that they are responsible for developing new knowledge for the field and the practitioners' claim that these theories run counter to established practices that are woven into the fabric of school life. No easy resolution exists for this dilemma because so few conversations are held about the vexing and complex differences in status and power that still exist between university faculty and school-based faculty. Although asking preservice teachers to engage in action research projects that are collaboratively negotiated may be one way to facilitate these conversations within a school, Noffke (1997) commented that "much work is clearly needed in articulating a practice of action research that would strive toward a profession of teaching that reaches beyond itself into broader social issues" (p. 328).

Another issue that concerns us in teacher education is how much emphasis should be placed in the preservice curriculum on preparing the students to assume a leadership role in the school, when their primary preoccupations center on learning how to develop good lesson plans that enhance their students' understanding of the content, undertaking both traditional and alternative assessment, and developing classroom management skills that lead to a well-functioning classroom. The problem is complicated by the fact that teacher education is attracting more and more people who are seeking a second career change, seasoned professionals who already possess considerable leadership skills, in sharp contrast to 20-year-old undergraduates who may have had few experiences that enhanced their leadership abilities. How much is it reasonable to expect students to learn in 1 or 2 years, before we put them to the test by giving them their own classroom to manage, especially in almost impossible circumstances in some districts? If the curriculum is to include a stronger emphasis on building leadership capacity at the preservice level, then we need to find ways in which students can be exposed to experiences that will give them this opportunity. In many states, the teacher education program now includes a 1-year internship onsite in a school where the preservice student is given a multitude of experiences. Cooperative agreements could be worked with school districts whereby students serve as apprentice teachers for the first year and are mentored both by an experienced teacher and an administrator. Such a model would return the administrator to the role of becoming more involved with learning and instruction issues, rather than just focusing on management and budgetary concerns. However, unless some of these managerial tasks are reassigned to other personnel within the school, the principal is likely to become overburdened with yet another task added to an already extensive list.

Administrator Cooperation

I noted earlier in this chapter that the involvement of administrators was critical for creating conditions within the school that made it easier for teachers to conduct action research. One of the greatest contributions is time—time for teachers to meet as a team, time away from class to observe each other's classes, time for professional development activities both inside and outside the school. One of the often-cited differences between American and European and Asian schools is the time allocated for teachers in the latter two environments for joint planning of curriculum and instruction—often as much as 2 hours per day. This idea runs directly counter to U.S. expectations that teachers should spend all their time in the classroom with their students, and few schools have the funds to hire additional staff to monitor students' activities while the teachers are engaged elsewhere. This situation is one that potentially could involve creative solutions such as using preservice students as interns to work with classroom students, but such a solution depends on having school administrators who are willing to take risks in developing innovative ways to free teachers' time, as well as on having university faculty who are willing to spend more time in classrooms in teaching, rather than research, activities. In the Goals 2000 project, the grant funds enabled the principals to release the teachers to meet as a group outside school, and the real challenge will be for them to find ways to continue the initiatives begun at their schools without outside funding.

A second issue that has become more prominent now that we have moved to an extended placement model using action research is the issue of how cooperating teachers are selected within a school. In the past, our placements were generally made through a district's central office, where the staff maintained a list of teachers who were willing to have a student teacher. Although we found many excellent teachers this way, we also encountered teachers who hadn't rethought and/or changed their pedagogical strategies in years, but who found favor with the administrative staff. Now that we have shifted our emphasis to having preservice students enter the classroom earlier in order to assist with an action research project, we are now hearing from teachers who had never before considered taking on a student teacher, but who now see this process as a way of revitalizing their professional development. At the same time, these teachers are often perceived by administrators as not the "best models" for preservice students to emulate, although no real reasons are stated. We suspect that many of these teachers are interested in action research as a way of developing a more authoritative voice about their practice but that they are also the ones who are least likely to conform to the status quo within a school. As these teachers seek us out, we do inform the school to maintain channels of communication, but it is also the case that school administrators will need to learn how to become more comfortable with teachers who exercise a greater degree of professional autonomy about the projects they want to take on to improve teaching and learning in their classroom. To do this, one of our goals is to develop a series of informational seminars for principals and BRIET liaisons to keep them informed of the need to recruit a different kind of cooperating teacher, one who is actively committed to reflecting on his or her practice and who is willing to change through involvement with action research.

University Faculty Cooperation

Long-lasting changes in the teacher education curriculum are not just dependent upon actions taken by BRIET staff; they are also dependent upon faculty cooperation within the Graduate School of Education and the larger university faculty. Although several faculty did choose to participate in rethinking the curriculum over the summer, not all who are involved in working with preservice teachers did so. A difficult dilemma confronting those who prepare professional educators is to how to work with faculty who want to maintain the syllabus they've constructed over time that is more appropriate for meeting the needs of higher education graduate students than it is for practitioners. The problem is further complicated by a lack of consensus, both within the GSE faculty, as well as on the national level, on just what constitutes the professional body of knowledge teachers need to have in order to become successful teachers. Without such an agreement, faculty tend to view the courses they teach as the ones that are necessary in order to protect the credit hours they earn for them.

A related problem is the subject of team teaching with clinical faculty. Some of the GSE faculty have been very receptive to this idea, but others have been noncommittal or noticeably cool to the idea. New assistant professors have a genuine and legitimate concern that their need to build a reputation as an excellent teacher (an area that is receiving more scrutiny) may be compromised by working with someone else. At the same time, joint teaching poses problems for department chairs to ensure an equitable teaching load among all faculty. Does a jointly taught course require the same degree of preparation as does one taught singly? Having taught both, I can attest to the fact that the jointly taught course often requires more work, but unless one has had the experience it's difficult to convince college administrators who equate individual credit hours with an adequate teaching load.

A third issue, one that impacts directly on faculty autonomy, is the sheer amount of time school/university collaborative activities consume, especially if the school is located far from the campus. A faculty member who chooses to become heavily involved with schools will undoubtedly find his or her time eaten away with commuting trips, attendance at school improvement meetings, conferences with teachers about their action research projects, and all the minutia of school life that people in the field routinely encounter. To faculty accustomed to scheduling their time to suit their convenience, such time-consuming involvement seems nightmarish, especially because in many cases people became college education professors precisely to escape this kind of life in schools. At the same time, unless one's entire research agenda is structured around working with schools, this level of commitment leaves virtually no time to pursue research agendas that may hold greater personal interest but are often ones that school people (and the general public) perceive as being disconnected to concerns within the field. Faculty within professional schools who raise this argument then become vulnerable to the charge that they are not being paid to pursue esoteric questions that may have little or no immediate relevance to improving practice in the field (see Chapter 2 for a critical discussion of the shift in values in schools of education between "my work" and "our work").

Power and Politics in the Change Process

Educational change is both difficult and exhilarating to accomplish. It's difficult because any change forces the advocates of change to confront the vested interests of the group or groups in power. Power is not a topic that most educators feel comfortable discussing (perhaps because they don't feel they have any), and interestingly enough, books on educational change typically do not focus on effective strategies for confronting those in power when they are resistant to change. While I agree with Fullan's quote of Marris's statement that "any innovation cannot be assimilated until its meaning is shared" (Fullan, 1991, p. 31), I would also argue that change cannot necessarily wait until complete consensus is reached on the shared need for change. In these cases, one can ask, What is the role of a leader in facilitating change when consensus has been sought but not achieved?

Two of the leading advocates of educational reform, Michael Fullan and Seymour Sarason, have different views of the role of power in fostering or blocking change. Fullan (1991) emphasizes the role of positive politics, which he defined as "focusing on a few important priorities by implementing them especially well, while keeping other potential priorities in perspective" (p. 347). In short, he believes that positive politics are a means to "use power to bring about improvements in our own immediate environment" (p. 348). Examining his statements in the context of teachers' action research, I believe he would support the idea that teachers should focus on taking actions within their classroom on aspects of teaching that they can directly control and leave larger questions to be pursued at a later time when more consensus has been reached, or when alliances have been forged with other groups that can facilitate change. Although Fullan acknowledges the difficulty in promoting and sustaining change, he appears more optimistic that once people recognize that "change is a process and not an event," and become committed to a long-term process that transforms themselves as much as the situation to be changed, reform is possible.

In contrast, Sarason is less sanguine about the possibility of change without acknowledging people's vested self-interests in reaching the desired ends through a given set of means. Sarason (1996) argues that

> From the standpoint of self-interest, those holding very different conceptions about educational decision-making face the same question on the level of action: What do I have to do to mobilize what kind of support to introduce and sustain the change? The inability to ask that question, because it is always embedded in a win-lose context suffused with passion and polarizations, prevents one from recognizing how narrowly one is defining self-interest. Self-interest has nothing intrinsically to do with selfishness or manipulativeness. It has a great dealt to do with how one defines, locates, and uses resources. (p. 90)

Sarason (1996) suggests that because educators fail to take this form of self-interest seriously, they cannot mobilize to take the necessary actions for change. Ironically, the movement toward enhancing teachers' sense of professionalism will only exacerbate the problem, because as Sarason noted,

One of the goals of professional training is to instill the sense of distinctiveness, if not uniqueness, about how one renders services and it is unprofessional for others who do not possess your knowledge and skills to determine your actions. Inherent in the concept of the professional is power, albeit circumscribed power. (p. 91)

I believe that when teachers become more involved in action research, they experience a greater sense of professionalism and develop a more authoritative voice about the efficacy of particular practices within the classroom. At the same time, I recognize that by engaging in actions that strengthen their professional beliefs about the efficacy of what they are already doing, they may become more resistant to changing their practice. Too often, the assumption of outside reformers is that the new innovation is a change for the better, when many teachers view change as a way of threatening established practices that work for them. How then is the problem that Sarason raised about self-interest and power to be resolved?

One answer is to listen more closely to the voices of teachers who have been involved in making substantive changes in their practice as a result of actions they have taken in systemic school reform. Wasley (1995) chronicled the experiences of teachers involved in school/university collaboration through the Coalition of Essential Schools. One teacher poignantly described what she had learned and her thoughts about how power is contested in schools:

Sometimes power struggles among staff interfered with our focus on pedagogical work. An uncomfortable feeling can settle on the entire staff. It's hard to remember to focus on what's fair for kids, not just what the adults feel comfortable with. When our expectation for students is that we will have very different, much more personal relationships, adults have to reshape their relationships as well. Sometimes issues of "political correctness" sidetrack us from the real issues of teaching and learning. It gets tough when we confuse ownership of the curriculum and decision making with the process of compromise and collaboration. (Wasley, 1995, p. 44)

This quote illustrates, as do the other situations described in this chapter, that power struggles exist on multiple levels: between K–12 teachers and university faculty, between administrators and teachers, between schools and universities, and even between faculty within a college of education in terms of those oriented to working more closely with schools and those more concerned with preserving traditional boundaries. Teacher researcher models that draw upon the concepts of action research see research intimately linked to practice in ways that allow teachers to reclaim their voice about appropriate models for teaching and learning. However, as Hargreaves (1996) noted, educational reformers must be prepared to listen to "multiple voices" and to resist the idea that a single innovation will fit all cases. More important, university faculty and practitioners who work within a collaborative framework must not only raise fundamental questions about the purposes and goals of education but also be prepared to undertake the difficult work of addressing them in the context of everyday life in schools. Those who challenge the conventional notion that educational theories can be developed apart from the realities of classroom and school life, and that educators at either level can remain distanced from their own practice, will have to demonstrate that their model leads to substantive change in schools in ways that have not been the case with the more traditional models. At the same time, the grinding realities of classroom life may temper their desire for emancipatory action and lead to the sobering realization that perhaps the only meaningful change that can happen is change in one's own practice. Carson (1990) described this concern well:

> Action research as a way of knowing becomes a hermeneutics of practice. A hermeneutics of practice tries to attend most carefully to interpreting the way we are with our colleagues and students in schools. It does not neglect the desire to make specific improvements, but it tempers this with the realization that because of our deeply ingrained habit of totalization (seeking certainty of knowledge or the "last word" on a topic) and prescription, we will easily be convinced to impose these improvements on everyone. An emphasis on interpretation attempts to resist and reform this habit, urging us to better develop our abilities to hear others. In the end, probably the most fundamental improvement that action research as a hermeneutics of practice attempts to make is the improvement of the quality of our life together. (p.173)

Improving the quality of life is the essence of education, yet it is a goal that is often subsumed under the concern for meeting curriculum standards, acknowledging the needs of diverse learners, managing a school budget within severe fiscal constraints, and all the myriad concerns that teachers and administrators face in the current school climate. The dialogue about reform must flow in two directions—not just from the university to the schools, but also back to the university—as to how teachers for those schools are being educated. Perhaps the best we can manage in present circumstances is to remain committed to the ideal of working out our differences within a collaborative framework that builds upon the strengths of both as we invent new models for professional education.

Notes

1. When BRIET was first developed, Associated Schools was the title given to schools that had a formal agreement with BRIET to provide 4 release days a year for any cooperating teachers to attend professional development seminars at the university. Each school has a teacher designated as a BRIET liaison whose assignment was to recruit teachers for placements and to hold field team meetings if more than one teacher in the school was serving as a cooperative teacher. In 1994-1996, there were 14 Associated Schools; 2 schools were added for the 1996-1997 year. Both urban and suburban schools were represented, as well as all three grade levels (elementary, middle, and high school). In the spring of 1997, we established a new model where these schools would now become Professional Program Schools, provided they agreed to take at least two student teachers. One of BRIET's future goals is to have all cooperating teachers drawn from these schools, because they have already demonstrated a commitment to becoming professional development schools by providing release time for teachers to engage these activities. In the case of the urban schools, this commitment represented a clear financial sacrifice because they were facing severe budget cuts in other program areas.

2. In cases where students evidenced no clear understanding of the action research process, or where cooperating teachers were reluctant to have the preservice teacher take a more activist role in the classroom by asking critical inquiry questions other than just simply observing the teacher, these students were given an alternative assignment.

3. The New York State Department of Education requires that prospective teachers have two student teaching placements. In BRIET, over the course of the academic semester, the first placement is for 9 weeks, and the second is for 7 weeks. We also balance them by urban/suburban locations and grade level.

4. Although many education professors are attracted to the idea that applying critical theory perspectives in schools will help increase students' motivation to learn because the issues are closer to students' concerns (e.g., a focus on class, race, and gender inequities in schooling), reports from the field suggest that their belief may be too optimistic. In several of Wasley's

(1995) accounts of urban teachers who were willing to "stir the chalkdust" through experimenting with innovative practices, the teachers noted that they first had to overcome tremendous resistance from students in doing anything different and that discussions of race or other sensitive subjects could only take place after the students had spent considerable time learning how to work cooperatively in groups. Peter McLaren (1989), a well-known critical theorist, has written an amusing account of his frustrating struggles as a teacher for 1 year in an urban school to make junior high students critical of social issues while dealing with the raging hormones and restlessness that characterize the behavior of early adolescents. Ironically, this realistic account is much less well known than his more theoretical works that advocate the importance of adopting a critical stance on the problems of urban schools. Brunner (1994), a former BRIET student, commented on how her attempts to empower her students in an urban school through a critical action research project initially led to the "death of idealism," although later she realized that "through the process of reflection and my attempts to interpret what happened, I found that I learned much that I had not seen before about the dynamics of change and its possibility. This knowledge I found ultimately empowering" (p. 42).

References

Ayers, W. (1992). Work that is real: Why teachers should be empowered. In G. A. Hess, Jr. (Ed.), *Empowering teachers and parents* (pp. 13-28). Westport, CT: Bergin & Garvey.

Brown, A. (1994). The advancement of learning. *Educational Researcher, 23*(8), 4-12.

Brunner, L. (1994). The death of idealism? Or, issues of empowerment in a preservice setting. In S. E. Noffke & R. B. Stevenson (Eds.), *Educational action research: Becoming practically critical* (pp. 31-42). New York: Teachers College Press.

Campbell, D. (1988). Collaboration and contradiction in a staff development project. *Teachers College Record, 90*(1), 99-122.

Carson, T. (1990). What kind of knowing is critical action research? *Theory Into Practice, 24*(3), 167-173.

Clift, R., Veal, M. L., Johnson, M., & Holland, P. (1990). Restructuring teacher education through collaborative action research. *Journal of Teacher Education, 41*(2), 52-62.

Cochran-Smith, M., & Lytle, S. (1990). Research on teaching and teacher research: The issues that divide. *Educational Researcher, 19*(2), 2-11.

Darling-Hammond, L. (1996). The right to learn and the advancement of teaching: Research, policy, and practice for democratic education. *Educational Researcher, 25*(6), 5-17.

Darling-Hammond, L., Ancess, J., & Falk, B. (1995). *Authentic assessment in action: Studies of schools and students at work.* New York: Teachers College Press.

Elliott, J. (1990). Teachers as researchers: Implications for supervision and teacher education. *Teaching and Teacher Education, 6*(1), 1-26.

Elliott, J. (1993). The relationship between "understanding" and "developing" teachers' thinking. In J. Elliott (Ed.), *Reconstructing teacher education* (pp. 193-207). London: Falmer.

Fullan, M. (1991). *The new meaning of educational change.* New York: Teachers College Press.

Giroux, H. (1988). *Schooling and the struggle for public life.* Minneapolis: University of Minnesota Press.

Hargreaves, A. (1996). Revisiting voice. *Educational Researcher, 25*(1), 12-19.

Kemmis, S., & McTaggart, R. (1988). *The action research planner* (3rd ed.). Geelong: Deakin University Press.

Kincheloe, J. (1991). *Teachers as researchers: Qualitative paths to empowerment.* London: Falmer.

Lieberman, A. (1990). (Ed.). *Schools as collaborative cultures.* London: Falmer.

McLaren, P. L. (1989). *Life in schools: Introduction to critical pedagogy in the foundations of education.* New York: Longman.

McNeil, L. S. (1989). *Contradictions of control.* London: Routledge & Kegan Paul.

Noffke, S. E. (1997). Professional, personal, and political dimensions of action research. In M. W. Apple (Ed.), *Review of research in education* (pp. 305-343). Washington, DC: American Educational Research Association.

Noffke, S. E., & Stevenson, R. B. (Eds.). (1994). *Educational action research: Becoming practically critical.* New York: Teachers College Press.

Oakes, J. (1985). *Keeping track: How schools structure inequality.* New Haven, CT: Yale University Press.

Palincsar, A. S. (1986). The role of dialogue in providing scaffolded instruction. *Educational Psychologist, 21*(1), 73-98.

Rudduck, J., & Hopkins, D. (1985). *Research as a basis for teaching: Readings from the work of Lawrence Stenhouse.* London: Heinemann Educational Books.

Sarason, S. B. (1996). *Revisiting the culture of the school and the problem of change*. New York: Teachers College Press.

Shulman, L.J. (1987). Knowledge and growth: Foundations of the new reform. *Harvard Educational Review, 51*, 1-22.

Spencer, D. A. (1996). Teachers and educational reform. *Educational Researcher, 25*(9), 15-17.

Valli, L., Cooper, D., & Frankes, L. (1997). Professional development schools and equity: A critical review of rhetoric and research. In M. W. Apple (Ed.), *Review of research in education* (pp. 251-304). Washington, DC: American Educational Research Association.

Wasley, P. (1995). *Stirring the chalkdust: Tales of teachers changing classroom practice*. New York: Teachers College Press.

Zeichner, K. M. (1991). Contradictions and tensions in the professionalization of teaching and the democratization of schools. *Teachers College Record, 92*(3), 363-379.

4

Preparing
Educational Leaders:
A Basis for Partnership

Stephen L. Jacobson

Whether one works in schools or schools of education, change has become a constant element in the lives of American educators. As illustrated in Chapters 1 through 3, the pressure for change has been persistent across various sectors of education for well over a decade. In most cases, the impetus for change has come from outside, but through a chain of events the need for change begins to be recognized, or is simply mandated, within schools themselves. In Helfrich's school district, for example, changing demographics caused by factory closings and an aging population led to a sharp decline in student enrollment, which, in turn, required that some schools in the district be closed. The recognition that the district would have to get by with less, but would be expected to achieve no less (or perhaps produce even more), caused school officials to revisit the central mission and operations of the district. Fear of job loss and "threats to traditional norms and ways of doing things" (Senge, 1994, p. 88) created insecurity, mistrust, and a resistance to change on the part of many teachers and administrators.

Similarly, Chapters 2 and 3 related a chain of events that moved from outside to within the university, specifically the Graduate School of Education (GSE) at the State University of New York at Buffalo (UB). Whether or not it was "manufactured" by partisan politics (Berliner & Biddle, 1995), the national debate over educational reform that began with *A Nation at Risk* in 1983 (National Commission on Excellence in Education, 1983), and continued in The Holmes Group trilogy (*Tomorrow's Teachers,* 1986; *Tomorrow's Schools,* 1990; and *Tomorrow's Schools of Education,* 1995), raised concern over the quality of education provided in our nation's public schools. These concerns led to focused criticism of the quality of preservice preparation received by teachers and administrators in institutions of higher education.

Challenges to traditional notions of scholarship were at the very heart of this criticism. Should college faculty, especially those at research universities where scholarship is prized, maintain a safe, antiseptic distance from the field for the sake of objectivity? Or should they immerse themselves in the hands-on, "rolled-up-sleeves work" of school improvement (Darling-Hammond, 1996)? When challenged, as Petrie notes, to change "my work" to "our work," the faculty of the UB's GSE were no less immune to insecurity, mistrust, and resistance to change than their public school counterparts. Quite simply, the press for change at all levels of public education has been matched by a persistent resistance to it.

This chapter continues the discussion about change and resistance to it. I argue that "we" (the university and the field) need to rethink the role of school leaders (whether administrator or teacher) and how they are prepared. To this end, there need to be changes in traditional power relationships that define schools; changes in commonly held, but potentially dysfunctional, conceptions of leadership; and changes in levels of collaboration between the university and the field. By working together on these issues, schools and schools of education have a unique opportunity for simultaneous improvement, and to build a profession "that is less balkanized" (Darling-Hammond, 1996). But make no mistake about it, these represent significant changes in well-entrenched ways of doing things at schools and schools of education. As Senge (1994) points out, resistance to change "is neither capricious nor mysterious" (p. 88). If attempted, the changes recommended will undoubtedly produce resistance because they will be viewed as threatening by some faculty members and administrators at both schools and schools of education.

I begin the chapter by examining three concepts I believe are fundamental to rethinking the role of school leaders and how they should be prepared: community, leadership, and shared vision. First, I describe and endorse Sergiovanni's (1994) conception of schools as communities, contrasting it with the more traditional model of schools as hierarchical organizations. With this communitarian model in mind, I propose that leadership in education be treated as a collective rather than an individual construct, with all educators prepared to assume leadership tasks when needed. Finally, I discuss vision building as also being a collective, rather than an individual, activity, with shared vision being the articulation of the unrealized, but collectively acknowledged, potential of a work group. One thing a "leader" does is to help a group articulate its collective potential. This section borrows extensively from Senge's (1994) work, *The Fifth Discipline: The Art and Practice of the Learning Organization.*

In the last section of the chapter, I describe and analyze a collaborative endeavor on the part of UB and several area school districts to rethink the role of school leaders and how they are prepared. Called the Leadership Initiative for Tomorrow's Schools (LIFTS), this program, now in its third year of operation, can also be traced to a national report on educational reform, *Leaders for America's Schools,* a report of the National Commission on Excellence in Educational Administration (University Council for Educational Administration, 1987). As Helfrich and Petrie describe in earlier chapters, the LIFTS initiative was spurred by a recognized need from school leaders in the field to redesign, improve, and participate in the preparation of future educational leaders in western New York. In this firsthand account of the development of LIFTS, I focus on several key design features of the program intended to foster the type of community building, collective leadership, and shared vision recommended in the paper.

Examining the LIFTS program provides a way to highlight the necessary changes that schools and schools of education ought to consider as they attempt to develop collaborative partnerships for leadership preparation. Although the terms *leadership* and *administration* are often used interchangeably in education, anyone who has spent any time in schools knows that not all school administrators are leaders and not all school leaders are administrators. I argue in this chapter that effective school change depends upon our ability to nurture the leadership potential of all educators, administrators, *and* teachers. Attempts to disentangle leadership from administration will be resisted because it represents an important shift in traditional power relationships in schools. Examining LIFTS provides an opportunity to review potential obstacles to implementation, and areas of confrontation, contestation, and resistance on the part of university faculty, students of administration, and the field.

Schools as Organizations or Communities?

In his classic study, *Gemeinschaft und Gesellschaft,* Tonnies (1887/1957) notes that a social relationship implies interdependence and that the will of one person influences that of others. The "collective will" can be either rational or natural; it can remain the same or undergo change. Tonnies used the term *gesellschaft* to describe societal types that operate through intention, in which dominant social relationships are characterized by rational calculation and exchange. In contrast, the term *gemeinschaft* describes more natural societal types that operate through sentiment, with social relationships characterized by fellowship, kinship, and neighborliness.

In an invited address to the American Educational Research Association, Sergiovanni (1994) aligned current definitions of organization and community with Tonnies's conceptions of gesellschaft and gemeinschaft, respectively. Organizations (gesellschaft), for example, are defined by explicit management structures and procedures, codified roles and role expectations, and the assumption that hierarchy equals expertise. "Those higher in the hierarchy are presumed to know more about teaching, learning, and other matters of schooling than those lower, and thus each person in a school is evaluated by the person at the next higher level" (Sergiovanni, 1994, p. 216).

Communities (gemeinschaft), on the other hand, emphasize informal relationships that rely on interdependence, with communities of "mind" emerging from "the binding of people to common goals, shared values, and shared conceptions of being and doing." (Sergiovanni, 1994, p. 219). Relationships in communities are intrinsically rewarding, and people are committed to one another through mutual agreement and sentiment. In contrast, organizations often require suppressing individual needs for the sake of achieving organizational goals; therefore, commitments are specified through formal contracts and policies—"rational calculation and exchange"—as members try to negotiate the best package of extrinsic rewards possible.

It should be obvious to even a casual observer that schools nowadays resemble organizations, not communities. Noting that "life in organizations and life in communities are different in both quality and kind," Sergiovanni (1994, p. 217) proposed that if the field of educational administration hopes to effect meaningful change in schools, it must replace the dominant organizational model with a "school as community" model. Whereas collegiality in organizations is fostered through structural arrangements (such as team teaching), and encouraged by appealing to personal self-interest (including monetary incentives), collegiality in communities "comes from within."

> If we were to change the metaphor for schools from organizations to community, and if we were to begin the process of community building in schools, then we would have to invent our own practice of community. This would require that we create a new theory of educational administration and a new practice of educational administration . . . more in tune with meaning and significance, and the shared values and ideas that connect people differently. And these new connections would require that we invent new sources of authority for what we do, a new basis for leadership. (Sergiovanni, 1994, p. 218)

Before considering the implications of a communitarian model as "a new basis for leadership," it is important to first understand why the organizational model came to be the dominant metaphor in public education.

From Communities to Organizations

During the 19th century, the common school sat at the center of the community. The school provided a place to congregate for social as well as educational events. It was a place in which community members took pride, and in many ways, the school was the community. During the 1890s, the needs and ethos of industry began to strongly influence the purpose and structure of American schools. It was a time of development and rapid industrialization. There was a pressing need for a large, but cheap, labor force that had a common language and work ethic, factors that would make supervision easier and less costly. Schools would serve as the cauldron for America's "melting pot." Rising immigration and birth rates resulted in more schools being built to accommodate the nation's growing school-age population. According to U.S. census data, there were just over 4 million youngsters between the ages of 5 and 17 years attending school in 1850—a figure that grew to almost 9 million in 1875, and 17 million in 1900, more than a fourfold increase in 50 years (Bureau of the Census, 1976).

This rapid growth created the need to adapt the types of specialized, hierarchical roles and explicit, standardized operating procedures that seemed to work so well in America's industrial sector. The mental model of the factory assembly line—each worker charged with a highly specific and carefully time-managed task, turning out products in an efficient, "scientifically" determined fashion—was extremely attractive to the American public. Therefore, principles of industrial scientific management were introduced to education early in the century (Taylor, 1911); with it came concerns for greater efficiency (Callahan, 1962). To create economies of scale, schools were centralized and consolidated. The total number of public school districts in the United States declined from approximately 130,000 in 1930 to 18,000 in 1970, whereas enrollments grew from 29 million to 51 million during the same time period (Bureau of the Census, 1976). In other words, fewer districts were serving many more youngsters and, over a 40-year period of consolidation, the average school district saw its student enrollment grow from a little more than 200 to just under 3000!

As districts grew larger, they became more hierarchically structured, and central office administrators expanded their role in the daily affairs of individual schools. Decision making over critical educational issues such as curriculum design and textbook purchases moved further from the class-room, teachers, and principals. As noted earlier, positioning on the governance hierarchy was assumed to reflect expertise. But when it came to issues of instruction and the needs of students in *their* schools, teachers and building-level administrators felt that they were the "experts." As a result, teachers and building-level administrators found themselves engaged in increasingly confrontational relationships with both the central office and each other. Because they are expected to execute district policies, including policies they may have had no say in developing and/or policies they know their faculties (and perhaps they, themselves) find objectionable, principals, as "middle managers," are in an especially vulnerable position in the organizational model.

From Organizations to Learning Communities

Imagine, instead, a less "Taylorized" school system with a relatively flat governance structure that recognizes expertise wherever it exists. Helfrich's effort to develop common goals and shared values (described in Chapter 1) was an attempt to foster mutual interdependence through the recognition of teacher expertise. Allowing teachers greater involvement in decisions that directly affected them provided them access to more information and a chance to better understand key issues under consideration. Moreover, it offered them the opportunity to exercise leadership and the possibility of reaching consensual agreement, which reduced the need for principals to enforce unpopular rules. Firmly entrenched power relationships that undergird "traditional norms and ways of doing things" can be altered by reallocating authority and control in this manner. But no less important than the redistribution of power is the fact that a more generalized appreciation of individual and collective expertise is likely to make work more intrinsically rewarding for employees whose knowledge is given voice.

> Material affluence for the majority has gradually shifted people's orientation toward work—from what Daniel Yankelovich called an "instrumental" view of work, where work was a means to an end, to a more "sacred" view, where people seek the "intrinsic" benefits of work. (Senge, 1994, p. 5)

One can see in Helfrich's discussion that, for some, the school had become a more "communitarian" organization. When Helfrich states that "pride was back," the implication is that a very powerful intrinsic reward was once again available to the members of that educational community. But this change in orientation depended upon two other key elements: (1) a different conception of school leadership and (2) the development of a shared vision.

Collective School Leadership

In his influential work, *The Fifth Discipline: The Art and Practice of the Learning Organization,* Senge (1994) argues that although individual learning is necessary, the team is the basic unit in organizational learning, and organizational learning is critical for continued success. Teams must be encouraged to share and test new ideas and insights, so that they may become part of a common knowledge base. BRIET's work with preservice and experienced teachers and the Goals 2000 Project reported by Emihovich suggest that action research is an approach that is especially appropriate for encouraging collective inquiry in schools. Collective inquiry such as this can produce generative learning that has the potential to outlive the contributions of any one individual, no matter how outstanding the person. For example, the use of planning and design teams and the quest for collective improvement continue in Helfrich's district well after his retirement.[1]

Facilitating the transition of individuals into teams of learners requires a new type of leadership, leadership that encourages a free flow of ideas and information as no one individual can be expected to be "all-knowing." To capitalize on the collective strengths of a team, a leader must be willing to forgo some measure of control. Relinquishing control is an act that engenders mutual trust—trust *of* the team and trust *by* the team. Leadership no longer resides solely with a single individual, but instead becomes a collective construct with different individuals and/or teams assuming leadership responsibility as needed. Contrast this notion of collective leadership with Senge's (1994) description of the more prevalent conception of "successful managers" in most organizations today:

> Being a successful manager means being decisive, being "in control," knowing what is going on, having answers, and forcefully advocating *your views* [emphasis added]. (p. xvi)

This conception of leadership stresses the will of one person over that of the collective, and Senge (1994) contends that this approach persists because "most managers find collective inquiry inherently threatening" (p. 25). But think of the burden, and ultimately the stress, created by having to feel that as the designated "leader," you have all the answers and are always in control. Principals are especially vulnerable to this type of pressure, feeling that they have to convince parents, teachers, and their supervisors in central office that they are decisive and in charge. Such self-inflicted stress can be exhausting. Leaders who feel they always fly at the front of the flock would be wise to study a formation of migrating geese. To avoid exhausting any one member of the flock, birds rotate continuously through the lead position on the vee. Every member of the flock has the potential to lead, and so this moment's follower becomes the next moment's leader.

> The organizations that truly excel in the future will be the organizations that discover how to tap people's commitment and capacity to learn at *all* levels in an organization. (Senge, 1994, p. 4)

Imagine a school characterized by teachers assuming leadership roles that capitalize on their particular areas of expertise when the need arises. The exertion required to lead a school, or school district, through the stiff winds of change would no longer rest solely on the shoulders of a single person. Instead, leadership would be shared collectively by a significant number of faculty, parents, support staff, and other members of the larger school community. Rather than reinforcing traditional power relationships by forcefully advocating a *personal vision* and requiring others to "buy in," Helfrich opted instead to tap the leadership potential of individuals throughout the district, recognizing that "effective progress can start in the middle as well as at the top of organizations" (Senge, 1994, p. xix). By encouraging people to participate and assume leadership in the change process, Helfrich's approach gradually reduced resistance. Change was now viewed as the way to create new opportunities, forge new relationships, and hopefully, realize a *shared vision.*

> When there is a genuine vision (as opposed to the all-too-familiar 'vision statement'), people excel and learn, not because they are told to, but because they want to. (Senge, 1994, p. 9)

Building a Shared Vision

The final ingredient needed to change schools from hierarchically run organizations to collectively led communities is the development of a shared vision.

> The practice of shared vision involves the skills of unearthing shared "pictures of the future" that foster genuine commitment and enrollment

rather than compliance. In mastering this discipline [building shared vision], leaders learn the counterproductiveness of trying to dictate a vision, no matter how heartfelt. (Senge, 1994, p. 9)

In addition to "unearthing shared 'pictures of the future,' " a shared vision provides an articulation of a collective potential. We have within us all both idealized pictures of the future, and those we believe are truly within our grasp. The same tension can exist for a school. There are ideal, but probably unrealistic, images of the future, and there are also scenarios that most would agree are possible. If there is general agreement about the desirability of an idealized future, the disparity between the ideal and the real can be the creative tension that focuses commitment. For example, an often-repeated objective of Goals 2000 is that all American students will meet world-class standards in math and science. This is a laudable goal—certainly one worth striving toward. Yet many seriously question whether this goal is really attainable for all students any time soon. Nevertheless, it presents a desirable goal against which to measure progress. Fostering genuine commitment, therefore, requires the articulation of both an idealized and realistic future, with the emphasis on the latter. As noted previously, this perspective contrasts sharply with the more common notion that vision is something a "leader" espouses, and others are encouraged, persuaded, coerced, or otherwise compelled to follow.

Helfrich's experiences provide insight into building a shared vision. But Helfrich's reminiscences (see Chapter 1) also indicate that the vision that emerged in his district was not a vision shared by the university. In fact, the opportunity to develop a realistic picture of the future that could have been shared by the district and the university never materialized because repeated attempts to align activities across institutions proved unsuccessful. The inability to bring these parties together is symptomatic of a rift in the perspectives of the university and that of the field. Petrie's distinction between perceptions of "my work" versus "our work" can be applied to faculty in public schools as well as the university. These differing perceptions explain some, but not all, of the impediments to university-district collaboration and partnership, particularly with regard to the preparation of school leaders.

Impediments to University-District Collaboration

A fundamental problem with the formal preparation of school leaders is that institutions of higher education often view their educational administration programs as little more than revenue generators. With more than 500 institutions offering coursework in school administration across the

United States, these programs are producing an oversupply of aspiring administrators, which appears to be insensitive to the actual demand for administrators in many parts of the country (Bliss, 1988; Jacobson, 1990). For more than two decades, western New York has had seven certification programs (three private institutions and four associated with the State University system). Bliss's (1988) data indicated that in New York there were five certified individuals for every administrative position, not counting the incumbent. No less troublesome than this "certification mill" mentality is the fact that course offerings in many programs often reflect the research and entrepreneurial interests of individual faculty members, rather than "real" issues and problems of school practice. As a result, we are preparing far too many people poorly, and significant pre- and inservice needs of school leaders are being neglected.

Preparing educational leaders is simply too important an activity to leave to the university. It is a task that must be shared by the university and the field, because if schools and schools of education are to change to meet the pressing challenges of the next century, then so too must the way we prepare those who will lead them. Preparing educational leaders can provide a meaningful basis for university–school district partnerships.

A Collaborative Approach
to the Preparation of School Leaders

What I have tried to develop to this point is that meaningful school change depends upon changing current conceptions of schools as organizations, school leadership, and vision. But where to start? I suggest we start with the preparation of school leaders because it is the quickest way to infuse these new conceptions into our educational system. If future school leaders (i.e., those individuals who have been identified by their colleagues as having leadership potential) come to share these new perspectives, they will become the agents of change in their own workplaces.

Before considering what a new, collaborative approach to leadership preparation might look like, we need to first examine the current state of administrator preparation. According to the *Leaders for America's Schools* report (University Council for Educational Administration, 1987), university preparation programs had a number of serious problems as they entered the 1990s. Heading a list of major deficiencies were a lack of collaboration with school districts; a lack of sequence, modern content, and clinical experiences; a lack of relevance to the demands of the job; a lack of systematic professional development for experienced administrators; a lack of leader recruitment in schools; and a lack of minorities and women in the field. A nationwide survey of administrators conducted by *Executive Educator* provided empirical support for many of these perceived deficiencies (Heller, Conway, & Jacobson, 1988). The survey revealed that half (51%) of administrators rated their training as either fair or poor, and 46% stated that program requirements were not sufficiently rigorous to meet the demands of the job. For 61% of the respondents, their on-the-job training was the most beneficial element of preparation, while only 7% viewed their university studies as most significant. It appears that it isn't until they are in the field that most administrators feel they get the training they need.

In 1989, UB's educational administration faculty began to consider program revisions. Having been named the nation's outstanding certification program in 1981 by the American Association of School Administrators (AASA), UB's program had remained relatively unchanged for over a decade. Although concern about program quality provided the initial impetus for redesigning the program, the real issue confronting the faculty at UB was declining student enrollments. An analysis of enrollment trends and program requirements of the seven preparation programs that serve the region revealed that the main obstacle to study at UB was the requirement of a full-year, full-time clinical internship. During the 1960s, the Ford Foundation had sponsored an experiment that provided stipends for students who participated in an administrative position for an academic year. Although paid internships had become increasingly rare, UB's requirement remained because the value of an in-depth clinical experience seemed like sound practice. Students, on the other hand, increasingly selected those programs whose internship requirements were less rigorous than UB's. For example, one SUNY program in the region requires a one-semester, part-time internship of 20 hours per week, 5 hours of which are credited for work done at home. Only half of the remaining 15 hours per week must be spent in administrative activities while students are in session. In other words, their internship requirement was less than one fourth as time intensive as UB's. For students, a part-time internship allowed them to retain their regular teaching positions (and with it their regular salaries), while taking on administrative tasks before and after school, during lunch, and during preparation periods. It is perhaps not surprising that the number of students applying to UB's program fluctuated, but remained relatively low during the 1980s. Between 1980 and 1984, enrollments dropped from 8 to 2 students per year; increased for the next 3 years, averaging almost 11 admissions per year; but once again declined to only 2 in 1989.

After several meetings and a 2-day retreat, the faculty decided to modify the internship requirement by halving it from 1 year full-time to either one semester full-time or 1 year part-time. By making this requirement less rigorous, UB became more competitive within a very short time. Enrollments grew rapidly, increasing to 14 in 1990, and averaging more than 10 students per year through 1996.

Besides loosening the internship requirement, there were other program changes, but these were minor adjustments in course titles and sequencing—modifications that can best be described as tinkering. It is important to note that these efforts at program redesign were conducted with relatively little input from colleagues in the field. In light of the NCEEA's expressed concern about the lack of collaboration with school districts, this insular effort might be interpreted as academic arrogance. Our faculty was charged with preparing school administrators, and we had been recognized for superior performance in the past. If there was a problem, it was not our problem. The problem was with the other programs, and with the fact that districts were not willing to pay for administrative interns. For Senge, the faculty's behavior reflected an all-too-common organizational learning disability: the tendency to see a problem as being "out there," as being someone else's problem. The faculty decided to accommodate these problems by making a few changes—changes with which *we* were comfortable. If the changes attracted more students, the central criteria by which success would be measured, everything would be fine. As it turned out, the changes did produce an upturn in enrollments, yet everything was not fine. While we were unilaterally easing clinical requirements to make the program more marketable, there was a growing perception among local practitioners that aspiring administrators needed more, not less, hands-on experience if they were to be adequately prepared to cope with the changing realities of public education. Our lack of communication with the field was soon to be redressed.

The Impetus for LIFTS

As described in Chapters 1 and 2, the impetus for LIFTS began in 1991, just 2 years after the educational administration faculty redesigned the certification program. There was concern by local school officials that the quality of applicants being considered for administrative positions did not match the demands of the job, especially for the principalship. When positions opened, districts had no problem recruiting an adequate supply of candidates, because area preparation programs continued to graduate a surplus of certified administrators. The problem that schools were experiencing was a lack of "quality" candidates. Simply put, while the *Leaders for America's Schools* report was recommending that preparation programs prepare "fewer, better," in western New York, we were preparing "a lot, poorly."

A task force composed of superintendents, their representatives, and UB faculty met regularly for more than 2 years. These meetings produced a new approach to preparation that would focus more on developing leadership and leadership skills than on training managerial techniques. The terms *leader* and *administrator* would not be used interchangeably in this new program. It was the task force's intention to treat leadership as a collective characteristic, so that the "leaders" we prepared, whether administrators or teachers, would

- Focus on the teaching-learning process
- Encourage and demonstrate risk taking and flexibility
- Encourage and demonstrate an appreciation for diversity and a commitment to equity
- Employ reflection and inquiry as constant components of practice
- Act in ways that are informed by the outcomes of systematic inquiry and moral deliberation

After reaching consensus about these guiding beliefs in May 1992, the task force moved quickly to translate them into a set of practices that would guide the development of the LIFTS curriculum. It was clear to all involved that school districts could no longer allow institutions of higher education to be the sole arbiters of best practice in leadership preparation. The members of the task force agreed that the traditional approach of discrete, university-based, discipline-based, and role-based courses was not sufficient for preparing future school leaders. Over the next 2 years, the task force developed an alternative program built around the following innovative design features:

- District participation in candidate recruitment and selection
- Candidates studying in cohort groups
- An integrated curriculum organized around problems of practice
- A full-time paid administrative internship served in two different districts during the second year of the program
- The assignment of an experienced school leader to serve as a mentor for each LIFTS cohort member

The first LIFTS cohort of nine members began in the summer of 1994, seven of whom completed the program in May 1996. The two individuals who dropped out did so early in the program when they realized that the rigors of this new form of preparation were more than they had anticipated. The second and third cohorts of seven and eight members, respectively, were admitted in 1995 and 1996.

Key Design Features

After almost 3 years of working with LIFTS, I feel that only now can I begin to explain how key design features help promote community, collective leadership, and shared vision building among cohort members. I have also begun to understand the resistance that these changes have produced. Next, I describe briefly the benefits and problems created by each design feature.

District Participation in
Candidate Recruitment and Selection

Recall that communities rely on interdependence that develops from common goals and shared values, with parties committed to one another through mutual agreement and sentiment (Sergiovanni, 1994). Having worked long and hard for 3 years to articulate a set of shared beliefs about leadership, and to design a program that would foster those beliefs, a sense of community had arisen among members of the task force. We furthered this sense of community by sharing the responsibility of identifying, developing, and supporting future educational leaders. Unlike most programs, where candidate self-nomination is the norm and selection is based almost exclusively on academic credentials, LIFTS candidates are recruited and nominated by colleagues and/or supervisors who recognize their leadership potential, insightful understanding of teaching and learning, effective communication skills, and ability to work in collegial groups, in addition to their academic ability.

By the spring of 1993, the task force felt the program was ready to begin operation, and applicants were recruited for the first cohort to start that summer. Unfortunately, although the participating districts were eager to start the program, an adequate pool of candidates could not be found. Our unsuccessful attempt at recruitment surfaced a number of problems. First, it became clear that selection by district nomination was viewed with suspicion by some potential candidates who felt that this would simply replicate the current style of administrative leadership, and thus favor those candidates who had displayed fealty to central office administration. Individuals who exhibited leadership by challenging current practices might stand less of a chance of being nominated, particularly those with close ties to the union. Before this problem surfaced, we had created a category of "at-large" candidates who would not be supported financially by their home districts, but instead by the pooled resources of districts seeking the services of administrative interns. Although we had instituted this designation to increase the number of districts and students participating in the program, it was our hope that potential candidates might view at-large support as helping to remove the onus of "favoritism" from their LIFTS involvement. At-large candidates still have to come highly recommended, but the recommendations can come from outside their own district. During the first 3 years of the program, there have been two such at-large candidates.

A more general problem was the fact that many prospective administrators are not risk takers; therefore, they were reluctant to enter a new program until they knew more about it. We realized that although we had solicited representation from district administrators and university faculty, we had not included teachers in any of our planning sessions. Although it had been our desire to broaden the participant base in our program redesign, we had not really changed traditional power relationships, so it should not have been surprising when some aspiring administrators responded to the program with mistrust. This seemed to be especially the case for men, who were looking for some assurance that LIFTS was more likely to enhance their future position in the job market than traditional programs. The overrepresentation of men in administrative positions reported in *Leaders for America's Schools* (University Council for Educational Administration, 1987) suggests that the existing system was working quite nicely for them. Only a few men applied for district support, and those who did were markedly less qualified than their female counterparts. As a result, our first cohort was entirely women, and of the first 22 participants in LIFTS, only 5 have been men.

After our initial false start, we tried once again to recruit candidates in the spring of 1994. If we were to get the program off the ground, mutual commitment would be essential. Four school districts agreed to sponsor candidates and we ran a series of informational meetings for potential cohort members. Helfrich's district was one of the first to commit to the program, but it was unable to find a candidate because many of those teachers with the most potential were already exercising leadership on school planning and design teams. At least for some teachers, it appeared that the district's success at broadening participation in decision making had reduced their interest in assuming traditional administrative positions. The district decided instead to sponsor an African American teacher from the Buffalo City School District, recognizing that although the racial demographics of the student body were changing, the demographics of the teacher and administrator workforce were not. This decision aligned with one of the principal missions of LIFTS, which is to promote greater diversity in educational leadership through the identification and recruitment of outstanding women and minorities. Of the first 22 participants in LIFTS, 17 (77%) were women, and 7 were (32%) minority (6 African Americans, and 1 Hispanic).

Candidates Studying in Cohort Groups and Having Mentors

Incoming LIFTS candidates work as a cohort group for the entire 2-year program, which includes two 3-week summer sessions. The cohort model was selected explicitly to build a sense of community and to foster an understanding of collective leadership among members of the group. A cohort's work begins the first summer by focusing on team building. With the first group, we thought we could build team morale through an intensive program of shared experiences. But over the course of the first year, we found that although shared experiences do build familiarity amongst a group of individuals, team building and the development of community are not assured without a process around which to focus these activities. The first cohort often struggled at reaching consensus, particularly over contentious issues that emerged from their year-long problem-based study (a charter school proposal to be discussed in the next section). When conflict arose, usually the only voices heard were those that were the loudest.

By the summer of the second year, we realized the need to integrate facilitator training into LIFTS preparation. The /I/D/E/A/ model had proven successful for team building in Helfrich's district (see Chapter 1), so on the basis of his recommendation, the second cohort began the program with a weeklong training session, where they were joined by the first cohort, then entering its second year. The cohorts used the next 2 weeks of the summer session to practice their group processing skills. Using the /I/D/E/A/ model, cohort members shared the responsibility of facilitating classes, making sure that all members were actively involved and that all their voices were heard. Asked during the program's ongoing assessment interviews to articulate the factors that most influenced their preparation, responses included:

> The people within the cohort. Going through it with them and watching us grow and change and interact with each other and challenging

different beliefs and statements and making you articulate what it is you really believe.

The cohort has, I think, really helped me to grow in terms of leadership. There's been a support system, but a tough support system. (Doolittle, 1996)

In fact, the influence of the cohort model has had such a strong effect on this first group that they continue to meet regularly, seeking ways to serve subsequent cohort groups and sharing insights gained about leadership upon their return to the field (four were appointed to administrative positions upon completion of the program).

One other LIFTS design feature is that each cohort member is paired with an experienced school leader who serves as a mentor. Mentors make themselves available to guide and support their protégés. Cohort members are encouraged to seek out their mentors for advice and to explore alternatives should questions or problems arise. Because LIFTS students work as a cohort, their mentors have opportunities to meet and interact with other cohort members, thus creating a network of experienced practitioners available to all in the group. This network proved to be especially useful during their internships, when cohort members were struggling with new roles and responsibilities. Although it is not prohibited, cohort members and their mentors generally do not come from the same district. We believe that a freer flow of ideas can take place when the parties have no fear of retribution for things said about their own district. We also see this interdistrict exchange as a broadening experience for both parties.

Integrated Curriculum Organized Around Problems of Practice

Rather than having students take a collection of discrete, discipline-based courses (e.g., philosophy or economics of education) or role-based courses (e.g., the principalship or school business administration), the task force decided that LIFTS cohort members would focus on contextualized problems of practice. The first cohort, for example, spent two semesters developing a proposal to redesign an urban elementary school. In April 1994, the board of education in Wilkensburg, Pennsylvania, had issued a request for proposal to redesign and run one of its schools, Turner Elementary School. Wilkensburg is a small urban district bordering Pittsburgh. It is a district experiencing the ravages of urban decay such as the loss of local business, dropping real property values, and crack dealing. Parents were pulling their children out of the district's schools and sending them to private schools or using relatives' addresses to get them into Pittsburgh's public schools. With the district's permission, LIFTS was allowed to submit a noncompetitive proposal well after the closing date, and the Turner School was free to use any innovative ideas they found in the proposal. The contract to run Turner Elementary was eventually awarded to Alternative Public Schools [APS] of Nashville, Tennessee, but many elements of the LIFTS proposal mirrored those in the winning proposal.

Although we knew the cohort could not actually run the school, we undertook this school redesign to better understand educational reform in light of real constraints. As the proposal developed, various issues became the focus of group discussions, including multicultural infusion in the curriculum, authentic forms of assessment, teacher empowerment, restructuring the school day and year, action-oriented reflective practice, children at risk, nonadversarial collective negotiations, the changing role of the principal, school-community-business collaborations, teacher recruitment, selection and socialization, staff development, and facilitating change. Working closely with the instructors, one from the university and one from the field, the group decided how best to examine each issue. Would the most meaningful approach be readings, lectures, visitations, videos, simulations, case studies, or some combination of the aforementioned? The cohort also visited the district and met with the acting superintendent, school board members, parents, union officials, the principal, and a teacher from Turner, in order to understand its social, economic, and educational context.

One of the most contentious issues for the cohort was the personnel option made available in the request for proposal. Specifically, the grantee could use Turner's existing faculty or bring in a new principal and an entirely new teacher workforce. Discussions about this provision were among the group's most heated and transformative of the entire experience. Being teachers themselves, cohort members were sympathetic to the plight of the teachers at Turner. Their first reaction was to recommend rehiring the existing staff. But because the school's student population was overwhelmingly African American, and the teacher force predominantly White, some questioned whether they needed to create a better racial balance, even if it meant replacing highly competent White teachers. The ensuing debate began to split the group along racial lines, with the four White cohort members arguing that competence, not race, should determine who would work at Turner. They wanted a selection policy that would be "color-blind." The three African American cohort members countered that a lack of educator role models of African descent perpetuated a racial imbalance between students and teachers that is all too common in urban schools. They offered reflections from their own educational experiences to make their point. As a result, the group crafted a selection policy based primarily on competence, but one which treated race as a relevant factor.

> Transformation occurs as the reformer feels the pain of the people oppressed. He [or she] is open to examining different standards of justice, thus understanding why certain development projects were rejected by the oppressed group. (Welch, 1991, p. 97)

Through shared experiences and meaningful interactions, cohort members began to confront their own racism as they worked to create a school that would serve the needs of the children, the community, and the teachers of Turner. Together, they began to understand how certain policies and practices that seem fair and eminently just to one group can be viewed as oppressive by another. "Emancipatory conversations are the fruit of work together; the result of alterations in relationships between groups" (Welch, 1991, p. 98). Subsequent interviews revealed the profound effect these "emancipatory conversations" had had on cohort members:

> It made me look at myself. I had to become introspective about what my belief system really was, what my practices really are, so I can back up what I say I believe. That was so wonderful! It was tough.

> I find myself challenging my own assumptions and my own beliefs, what I used to think were my own beliefs, as I talk to other people. (Doolittle, 1996)

These experiences helped cohort members develop and shape their personal educational platforms. Senge (1994) notes that "Leadership springs from deep personal conviction" (p. xvii). Yet how many educators have taken the time to carefully consider the values and beliefs they hold dear with regard to the role and purpose of education in a democratic society? We asked cohort members to do just that in developing their educational platform statements. Because the Turner proposal required the articulation of a vision statement for the redesigned school, preparing individual platform statements represented an important first step in attempting to build a shared vision.

As useful as this exercise proved to be, there were some drawbacks. First, the 10-hour round-trip drive between Buffalo and Wilkensburg made subsequent visits to the district unfeasible. We originally thought that distance would provide the advantage of objectivity, that is, we could look at the Turner school with clarity and no preconceptions. Instead, we felt far removed from the context that we had tried so hard to understand. Upon reflection, the group felt that this field-based exercise could have been more meaningful had it been conducted closer to home. As a result, the cohort I'm currently working with will be immersed in local school activities. It is this type of learning from one cohort to another that we feel is necessary to sustain the continued success of the program.

A second issue raised by the change from a traditional model of preparation to an integrated curriculum was a concern among members of the first cohort that they might not be adequately prepared. Toward the end of the first year, they wondered aloud whether their not having taken semester-long courses in school law or personnel, for example, put them at a disadvantage relative to students who had. Assurances from the clinical faculty and their mentors—that the trade-off between the type of decontextualized subject matter that characterizes traditional coursework and the model of learning to learn within the reality of the school workplace that they had practiced for over a year would ultimately prove beneficial—did little to allay their fears. In fact, it wasn't until cohort members were involved in their year-long clinical internships that they began to recognize the advantages of this holistic approach to instruction. Having focused from the very beginning of the program on the systemic nature of schools and schooling, rather than on its discrete parts, cohort members felt that they had a sense of the "big picture." In contrast, the interconnectedness of coursework is rarely made explicit in most administrator preparation programs; therefore, students are left on their own to try and put the pieces together during a short, fragmented clinical experience. Although they still had some reservations, the confidence of cohort members in their ability to lead grew markedly during their internships.

Another change of note is that the LIFTS program is nongraded. We assume that when we select an individual into the program, we have a collective responsibility to see that the person has a successful experience. Rather than nurture competition through the traditional grade-point system, we believe that cooperation is more likely to flourish in an environment where high quality is an expectation, but grades are taken out of consideration. Students revise papers until they and the faculty are satisfied with the product. An individual's strengths are recognized and weaknesses addressed, but not in relation to the relative strengths and weaknesses of other cohort members, a natural by-product of grades. Even if an individual chooses to leave the program, which has occurred twice, an important learning experience has still occurred, because the person has come to realize that the rigors of leadership development are more than he or she is willing to undertake.

Finally, the use of an integrated, "emerging" curriculum represents a fundamental change in the role of the professor. Toward the end of the first year, I began to realize the arrogance implicit in a typical course syllabus. Experienced educators are told what to do and when to do it, as if their own prior knowledge and wealth of experience is irrelevant. The first cohort and I found ourselves struggling to overcome deeply embedded expectations and power relationships of the classroom. During discussions the group looked toward me for direction. Much like principals who feel the need to "lead" even when they know they're not the most appropriate person at the moment, I initially felt compelled to respond. But realizing that I had to model collective leadership, and not just talk about it, I began to defer to the expertise of others in the room. I had never thought to regularly ask a group of students about what they thought needed to be done within the context of their own learning. I must admit to some resistance at first. I had a vague sense that I was giving away some of my "authority." But ultimately, the experience has been liberating for me and I hope for the cohort members as well. I have no doubt that we accomplished more that first year—and that the course material was more personally meaningful, when we undertook curriculum development collectively—than if I had simply done it alone.

Paid, Full-Time Internships in Multiple Sites

During the second year of preparation, each member of the cohort is placed in two different field sites as part of a 180-day clinical internship. The first placement is at the building level for 120 days, whereas the second 60-day experience can be either at the building level or central office, depending on the student's career aspirations. These placements involve activities in urban, suburban, and/or rural schools. The purpose of a full-year, full-time experience is to expose LIFTS interns to the daily realities of school administration and leadership, whereas the multisite approach is intended to expose them to different people, environments, policies, practices, and possibly, different styles of leadership.

To sponsor a candidate, a district takes on a financial obligation of approximately $20,000, with the bulk of this investment coming during the internship year.[2] The willingness of districts to assume an additional expense of this magnitude is where the "rubber hits the road" in terms of maintaining an ongoing university–school district partnership. Although they recognize the value of developing the leadership skills of their most talented individuals, and of having them experience full-time administrative internships, districts are hesitant to sponsor candidates because of the cost. With an abundance of preparation programs in the region, many school districts in western New York view leadership preparation as a no-cost item, as long as the programs continue to produce a steady supply of certified administrators, regardless of their quality. In fact, many districts actually capitalize on the rather lax internship standards described earlier by allowing teachers to satisfy their clinical requirements by taking on administrative tasks, such as summer school assistant principal, at no pay.

Assuming that a district is willing to sponsor a candidate, what guarantee does it have that the candidate won't take a position elsewhere? In other words, how can districts protect their investment? We've heard these questions often, and the only answer we can offer is that there are no guarantees. A district could obligate a sponsored candidate to 1 or 2 years of service in the district upon completion of the program, but a better approach is to provide candidates opportunities to maximize their newly honed talents. We also like to point out that the multisite requirement of a LIFTS internship means that a district has the opportunity to work with one or two talented candidates from other districts. Although we do not encourage districts to lure candidates away from one another, especially the wealthier suburban districts hiring candidates from the urban districts, one goal of the program is to improve the quality of the overall pool of future school leaders, wherever they ultimately practice.

Needless to say, having to pay for interns has produced considerable resistance to this new model of leadership preparation. Yet it is the interns themselves who actually subsidize much of a district's expense by taking a 1-year reduction in salary. Instead of their regular pay, cohort members receive a $30,000 stipend during their internship, which, for the first two groups, produced an average district savings of $14,900. The cost of providing a classroom replacement usually outstrips these savings, but because the substitute teacher is typically on a much lower salary step than the LIFTS candidate, the additional payroll cost has averaged only $16,700, for which the district gets a full year of administrative support from LIFTS interns. As with traditional programs, LIFTS candidates bear the full cost of tuition for this 36-credit program. If they move quickly onto the higher salary schedule of administrators, over time LIFTS graduates should be able to recover most of these expenses.

One last point about the cost of administrator preparation. Most districts in western New York currently have contractual provisions that pay teachers salary increments for graduate credit accumulation. For example, one local district pays $55 per credit. The completion of a 36-credit certification program would thus yield a $1,980 pay increase. Over the course of a career, a teacher who completed such a program would cost the district a substantial amount in additional salary, even if the district deemed them unqualified for an administrative position. Because most certification programs focus on managerial rather than leadership skills, if the person never leaves the classroom, the return to the district on this investment is minimal. As noted previously, school districts in New York have an abundance of these "papered people." In contrast, it is our hope that the focus on collective leadership that exemplifies LIFTS will have a genuine payoff to participating districts whether their candidates remain in the classroom, attain an administrative position, or create new types of leadership roles.

Where Do We Go From Here?

It is still too early to determine how successful LIFTS has been, but a preliminary assessment by Hickcox (1995) of the Ontario Institute for Studies in Education had the following words of praise and caution:

One of the more interesting aspects of the program, from an outsider's point of view, has been the effort to specifically tailor the program according to state-of-the-art thinking about what administrator and leadership training programs should be about. Lots of programs pay lip service to this, but LIFTS has actually made a serious effort to have its program reflect what both practitioners and serious scholars have been saying should be considered in training. (p. 3)

Throughout the report, we have alluded to issues related to finances for the program . . . the financial structure is quite fragile. The area of financing that I think should receive the most attention is support for the candidates. They do receive considerable support already for their internship year, but in most cases the program results in a decrease in resources for the individual on top of an increase in responsibility. One might argue that candidates should shoulder a good portion of the cost because they will be in line for higher paying jobs later in their careers. I don't think this is enough of an argument in today's world to convince many qualified candidates to make the commitment. (p. 11)

Clearly, the long-term success of LIFTS depends upon the extent to which participating districts and potential candidates view the program as a superior approach to leadership preparation.

The first cohort completed their internships in June 1996, and their supervisors' evaluations were outstanding. Four have already received administrative appointments—two in their own districts and two in other participating districts. The feedback from employing districts is that these LIFTS graduates are demonstrating mature, confident leadership that belies the fact that they are so new to their roles. Districts that have not participated are now requesting information and soliciting advice from participating districts about the costs and benefits of sponsoring a LIFTS candidate. In addition, we have experienced a steady increase in the number of inquiries from teachers interested in becoming cohort members. Prospective administrators are now less reluctant to enter the program because it appears that LIFTS participation may enhance an individual's position in the local job market. We have seen an increase in both the number and quality of men interested in LIFTS, and the participation of men has grown from 0 to 2 to 3 over the first 3 years.

It appears that the field is beginning to realize benefits from this collaborative program, but perceptions at the UB are less clear. There has been support from the dean, who has been willing to expend time and money to support LIFTS from planning to implementation. But not all GSE faculty are as supportive of making school improvement the central focus of "our" work. Changes such as an integrated curriculum, ungraded coursework, and coteaching with clinical faculty have met with some resistance. As Darling-Hammond (1996) notes, working with the field can be messy. Some academics feel a threat to their authority when working with people who have more practical experience. Simply arranging meetings and activities that involve people from the university and the field can be such a daunting task as to eat away at the time needed to accomplish "my" work—the research and publication that the university rewards. There are just a few of us at UB currently willing to take on this task. We need to find ways to invite more participation. As Emihovich suggests in Chapter 3, there exists the potential for greater coordination between LIFTS and BRIET, as leadership comes to be seen as a central element in the preparation of all educators. That said, one can also envision interactions with other educational professionals being prepared at UB including school psychologists, counselors, therapists, and so on. But each of these interactions will require changes in long-held policies and practices, changes that will in turn engender resistance.

As noted at the start of the chapter, demographic, economic, and societal changes challenge educational leaders to rethink schools and schooling, and to create learning communities that are more meaningful to the lives of students, teachers, and the larger public they serve. The challenge of creating communitarian organizations capable of building a shared vision and nurturing collective leadership requires a level of cooperation that does not exist at present. The university and the field can no longer operate within separate spheres, addressing goals that are often at cross purposes. Quite simply, the problems are too complex and important to leave to either one.

> Organizations work the way they work, ultimately, because of *how we think and how we interact.* Only by changing how we think can we change deeply embedded policies and practices. Only by changing how we interact can shared visions, shared understandings, and new capacities for coordinated action be established. (Senge, 1994, p. xiv, emphasis in original)

Notes

1. See Shipengrover and Conway (1996) for a detailed examination of 13 years of change in the Kenmore–Town of Tonawanda (Ken-Ton) Union Free School District, including the years subsequent to Helfrich's retirement.

2. During the first year of the program, districts pay an $1,800 fee per candidate plus replacement costs of approximately $1,500 for 20 released days (at $75 per day). Data from the first two cohorts revealed that excluding fringe benefits, the internship year was costing districts an additional $16,700 in payroll ($30,000 LIFTS intern stipend + $31,600 average teacher replacement salary - $44,900 average LIFTS candidate salary). In the case of two districts that did not replace their interns, they saved the difference between their candidate's regular salary and the $30,000 stipend. See Jacobson (1996) for more details about LIFTS financing.

References

Berliner, D., & Biddle, B. (1995). *The manufactured crisis.* Reading, MA: Addison-Wesley.

Bliss, J. (1988). Public school administrators in the United States: An analysis of supply and demand. In D. Griffiths, R. Stout, & P. Forsyth (Eds.), *Leaders for America's schools: Final report and papers of the National Commission on Excellence in Educational Administration* (pp.193-199). San Francisco: McCutchan.

Bureau of the Census. (1976). *Historical statistics of the United States. Colonial times to 1970, Part I Education* (Series H 412-787). Washington DC: U.S. Department of Commerce.

Callahan, R. (1962). *Education and the cult of efficiency.* Chicago: University of Chicago Press.

Darling-Hammond, L. (1996). The right to learn and the advancement of teaching: Research, policy, and practice for democratic education. *Educational Researcher, 25*(6), 5-17.

Doolittle, V. (1996). *Looking for leadership: Developing conceptions of leadership in an administrator preparation program.* Unpublished dissertation, State University of New York at Buffalo.

Heller, R., Conway, J., & Jacobson, S. (1988). Here's your blunt critique of administrator preparation. *Executive Educator, 10*(9), 18-22, 30.

Hickcox, E. (1995). *Early evaluation of the LIFTS program.* Unpublished report for the Graduate School of Education at the State University of New York at Buffalo.

Holmes Group. (1986). *Tomorrow's teachers: A report of the Holmes Group.* East Lansing: Author.

Holmes Group. (1990). *Tomorrow's schools: Principles for the design of professional development schools.* East Lansing: Author.

Holmes Group. (1995). *Tomorrow's schools of education.* East Lansing: Author.

Jacobson, S. (1990). Future educational leaders: From where will they come? In S. Jacobson & J. Conway (Eds.), *Educational leadership in an age of reform* (pp. 160-180). New York: Longman.

Jacobson, S. (1996). *Transforming the preparation of educational leaders through university/school district collaboration: The leadership initiative for tomorrow's schools (LIFTS).* Paper presented at the annual meeting of the American Education Finance Association, Salt Lake City.

National Commission on Excellence in Education. (1983). *A nation at risk.* Washington DC: U.S. Government Printing Office.

Senge, P. (1994). *The fifth discipline: The art and practice of the learning organization.* New York: Currency Doubleday.

Sergiovanni, T. (1994). Organizations or communities? Changing the metaphor changes the theory. *Educational Administration Quarterly, 30*(2), 214-226.

Shipengrover, J. A., & Conway, J. A. (1996). *Expecting excellence: Creating order out of chaos in a school district.* Thousand Oaks, CA: Corwin.

Taylor, F. W. (1911). *The principles of scientific management.* New York: Harper & Brothers.

Tonnies, F. (1957). *Gemeinschaft und gesellschaft* [Community and society] (C. P. Loomis, Trans.). New York: Harper & Row. (Original work published 1887)

University Council for Educational Administration. (1987). *Leaders for America's schools: The report of the National Commission on Excellence in Educational Administration.* Tempe, AZ: Author.

Welch, S. (1991). An ethic of solidarity and difference. In H. Giroux (Ed.), *Postmodernism, feminism, and cultural politics: Redrawing educational boundaries* (pp. 83-99). Albany: SUNY Press.

5

Educational Practitioners' Use of Research: Expanding Conventional Understandings

Robert B. Stevenson

Educational research is dismissed by some as irrelevant to educational practice, whereas to others it is essential for the improvement of education and schooling. Many practitioners and policymakers tend to the former view, whereas most researchers, of course, subscribe to the latter. Defenders of research usually argue that it creates new knowledge about teaching, learning, and the administration of schools that can then be applied to the improvement of educational practice (Borg & Gall, 1991). Critics, especially those expected to implement the new findings, complain that the knowledge and theory generated is not useful because it is "too theoretical" (meaning that is not sufficiently practical) or not relevant to the particular context in which they work. Consequently, the vast majority of educational practitioners view research as contributing to the advancement of theory, but not to the improvement of practice.

Although it must be acknowledged that the contribution of research to educational theory is easier to demonstrate than whether research findings have an impact on practice, given the many other influences that act on

AUTHOR'S NOTE: I wish to thank Stephen Brown, Catherine Cornbleth, S. G. Grant, and Barry Shealy for their helpful comments on earlier drafts of this chapter.

educational practice (Borg & Gall, 1991), universities must accept much of the responsibility for this situation. Practitioners' perception of research can be attributed not only to the kinds of research that historically have dominated the agenda of university researchers, which no doubt have been constituted and sustained by the higher status accorded original research that contributes to the development of educational theory, but also to the prevalent conception of the relationship of research-generated knowledge and theory to practice. In this chapter, I argue that the value or significance attached to research by practitioners is dependent not on their position or role in the educational system, but on how they view the purpose and use of research and its relationship to practice.

In the past and still much of the present, researchers, regardless of their particular methodological orientation, have assumed a "top-down" model of how theory and practice relate. This kind of model has been, until recently, epitomized by the education of doctors where one studies science for its all-encompassing truths and then learns to apply the science in practice with patients.[1] This model is also to be found in the social sciences, including education, where research-generated theory serves as a source of the knowledge base for preparation programs for teachers and school administrators who are expected to apply the most reliable and current knowledge about teaching and learning, or the management and leadership of schools to their classroom or administrative practice. This assumption about the relationship between theory and practice has influenced both the type of research conducted in education, as well as who has legitimacy for conducting research. Paradoxically, however, studies of decision making in teachers indicate that research knowledge is not a significant source for guiding teachers' practice (Huberman, 1983; Kagan, 1990; Richardson, 1994). This literature on how professionals think and make decisions about their practice and other literature on action and participatory research offer some important insights into alternative ways of viewing the relationship of research to practice.

The purpose of this chapter is to broaden the conversation on ways in which validated knowledge can be acquired and used by educational practitioners by examining the role that research or systematic inquiry can play in their professional lives. First, two approaches to using the products of research, by translating research findings into practice, are presented. These two approaches treat research findings as sources of either (a) guidelines for practice or (b) analytical or conceptual categories for thinking about practice (Doyle, 1987). Traditionally, the use or application of research findings generated by others, from research conducted "on" practitioners, has been treated as the only way in which practitioners are connected with research; that is, as the consumers or implementers of the products of research.

Second, besides using research findings, practitioners can also be involved in the generative phases of the research process. Such involvement can entail external researchers working collaboratively "with" practitioners in order to co-construct ways of viewing practice, or practitioners conducting research themselves (i.e., research "by" practitioners), either alone or in collaboration with others, as an integral part of practice. The former is commonly referred to as collaborative research, whereas the latter is often found under the label of action, teacher, or participatory research. In both cases, there is a recognition of the capacity of practitioners to contribute to the production of local or contextualized knowledge, although the extent to which practitioners are seen as generating formal or theoretical knowledge varies.

The final third of the chapter examines the implications of these different forms of practitioner use of research for preparation programs and the role of university researchers. Underlying these different forms of practitioner "use" of research are different views of how "theory and practice" and "knowledge and action" are related. Given that teacher and administrator preparation programs traditionally have been based on the assumption that educational theory should be applied directly to practice, the implications for such programs of the other ways of involving practitioners in research are then discussed. The different assumptions about the relationship between the researcher and the researched also have implications for the ways in which university researchers work with practitioners and the kinds of collaboration that might occur between universities and schools to improve educational practice. The chapter concludes by raising some challenges for university researchers and some issues in creating more democratic forms of collaboration in the production of knowledge and action for better schools.

First, however, I begin by defining what I mean by *research* and *theory*. Research can be defined as systematic inquiry that seeks to produce understanding or knowledge about perplexing and significant problems or questions. Systematic means that the inquiry is guided by a set of procedures, including principles or rules for evidence, that have been agreed upon by a community of researchers. It is some of the statistical procedures and rules for analyzing quantitative information that have contributed to a mystification of research and an assumption among many educators that all research must satisfy these procedures. Yet such procedures are relevant to only one kind of research, namely, that conducted within an empirical-analytic or positivistic tradition.

The mystification of research also can be attributed in part to the prevailing view of theory in Western society as constituting a high level of abstraction that is divorced from the realities of everyday life, and in part to the professionalization of knowledge such that the labor of knowledge production is confined to specialists. The origins of this dominant view of theory can be traced to the Greek philosophers who proclaimed the existence of a higher realm of reality or understanding that they saw as being occupied by theory. Consequently, theory is often used to mean something opposed to or apart from practice (Eraut, 1994), such as "the branch of a science or art that deals with its principles rather than its practice" (*Random House Dictionary*, 1980). The professionalization of the production of theory can be connected with the rise of scientific method and a definition of theory based on that method's testing of empirical propositions: for example, "a coherent group of general propositions used as principles of explanation for a class of phenomena" (*Random House Dictionary*, 1980).

Instead, in this chapter I adopt Michael Eraut's (1994) broader definition that "educational theory comprises concepts, frameworks, ideas, and principles that may be used to interpret, explain, or judge intentions, actions, and experiences in educational or education-related settings" (p. 70). As Eraut argues, this conception of theory recognizes not only the traditional notion of public theory (e.g., Kohlberg's theory of moral development, human capital theory, critical social theory) as a published system of ideas with an accompanying literature of elaboration, interpretation, and critique, but also private theories that are "ideas in people's minds which they use to interpret or explain their experiences" (p. 70). In the later case, the ideas may or may not be connected in any way to any publicly available theories, although their use may be tacit rather than explicit, but they must at least be capable of being explicated. Empirical research, therefore, is one—and only one—of several sources for generating theory.

Research Findings as Guidelines for Practice

The common perspective on the use of educational research views research findings as guidelines for practice that teachers and administrators can apply directly in their schools (Doyle, 1987). Process-product studies on teaching and associated field experiments on teachers' use of the results of these studies are an example of the application of research findings as guidelines for practice. Field experiments revealed that experienced teachers who volunteered to participate were able to use some of the information included in specifically prepared dissemination materials, but significantly, suggestions requiring substantial changes in existing practice were not used (Doyle, 1987).

Research that focuses upon teaching or school effects is usually advocated as being most suited to this application of findings. The types of questions addressed by this kind of research include the impact of particular interventions, such as teaching strategies or organizational practices, on student performance; specific behaviors or attitudes of teachers or administrators; and the relationships among teacher (or principal) characteristics, teacher (or principal) behaviors, and student (or teacher) outcomes, such as achievement or attitude (Popkewitz, 1986). As these examples illustrate, this approach to research attempts to identify constituent elements of classrooms and schools that are observable (or can be made observable) and connected to human behavior. Therefore, many argue that the accumulation of research findings with this focus can provide a resource for improving educational practices by isolating factors that can be manipulated by schools.

A number of epistemological assumptions underlie this empirical-analytic or positivistic view of research and its application or use. A first assumption is that knowledge claims are derived from empirical propositions and validated by a scientific method. In other words, knowledge claims are limited to observable phenomena (or phenomena for which observable constructs can be substituted), meaning that questions of intent and purpose tend not to be addressed. Furthermore, these propositional knowledge claims are assumed to be generalizable and applicable across different school settings and time periods. Another assumption is that knowledge, in the form of research findings, has an instrumental purpose in being directly informative in the making of a decision about practice. In other words, there is assumed to be a direct, linear relationship between propositions generated by researchers and their application to the improvement of practice because these propositions involve predictive statements such as "If X occurs, then Y will follow."

It is not only the texts from empirical-analytic studies, however, that are used as guidelines for practice. "Findings" from interpretive research, for example, which focuses on how educators make sense of teaching and schooling rather than on effective behaviors, also can be treated in this way. However, interpretive researchers do not assume that the knowledge or understandings generated are applicable to settings beyond those in which the research was conducted. And even when readers of the products of the research see some relevancy to their own context, these researchers do not assume that they will directly apply this knowledge but rather make their own sense of the research presented. The issue is how the results of research are used and not the kind of research that is conducted.

A major problem with this approach to knowledge use is that research

> findings do not translate into unambiguous prescriptions or blueprints for action to be followed mechanically by teachers. All propositions derived from research (or any other source for that matter) must be interpreted in light of particular circumstances and connected to specific occasions for application. (Doyle, 1987, p. 97)

The occasion for application includes the purposes for which particular knowledge or research findings are intended to be used. The goals or purposes of the practitioner or person implementing such knowledge influence its application, and they may be quite different from the purposes and set of questions guiding the researcher (Green & Chandler, 1990). Put simply, knowledge implementation is not a generic or linear process. Research on teacher thinking confirms that teacher planning and decision making do not follow linear prescriptions and propositions derived from research and theory (Richardson, 1994).

This perspective on the use of research, therefore, has limited utility. It is likely to be of most value for acquiring and implementing knowledge of specific, relatively straightforward techniques or practices whose application is relatively invariant of the particular context in which they are to be used, and that do not represent a substantial departure from a practitioner's existing repertoire of skills. As a result of this limited value, "support for the notion that theory derived from discipline-based inquiry can be directly applied to practice has dwindled over the last decade" (Eraut, 1994, p. 75). Many authors even argue that such a relationship is impossible (Hirst, 1979; McIntyre, 1980; Tom, 1980).

Research Findings as Analytical Constructs for Reflecting on Practice

Research findings, instead of being viewed as guidelines for practice, can serve as concepts or analytical constructs or categories that educators use to reflect on and analyze their practice, particularly to "help them grasp in descriptive and explanatory ways certain aspects of their work that were previously unaccessible" (Zeichner & Liston, 1996, p. 30). A study of teachers' responses to the research on effective instruction revealed that empirically derived propositions were treated by teachers merely as a piece of information to inform their own decision making rather than rules to be directly applied in their classrooms (Driscoll & Stevens, 1985). Other studies of teachers' curriculum planning and decision making indicate that new information and ideas are subjected to an intuitive test against the accumulation of personal experiences to determine if they match one's existing situation (Huberman, 1983; Toomey, 1977). In other words, new information is integrated with one's existing knowledge and schema for understanding teaching and interpreted in relation to the particular circumstances and occasion in which it is to be used (Stevenson, 1996). Significantly, the source of most of teachers' new information and ideas is not external authorities who have empirically tested the knowledge claims, but their own experiences of trial-and-error "experiments" and those of experienced colleagues (Huberman, 1983). In short, teachers appear to use information, whether it emanates from research or other sources, to reflect on classroom events and problems and to modify their pedagogical thinking.

This approach of translating research findings into analytical constructs or conceptual categories that are useful for practical theorizing about teaching and other kinds of educational practice has several epistemological distinctions from the first approach. Instead of knowledge having an instrumental (or means to an end) function, "use" involves "thinking about the evidence," and new evidence influences the user's working knowledge of the issues at hand (Kennedy, 1984, p. 207). A further contrast with the first approach to research findings is the recognition that not only can new knowledge influence an individual's point of view, but the individual's existing knowledge can influence the interpretation of new knowledge. Thus, knowledge is not static but constantly being constructed and reconstructed by the user.

This conceptual or interpretive use of knowledge reflects a recognition that educational practitioners work in a complex situation where most practices and circumstances are filled with a rich set of particulars (and even conflicting information) that researchers are unable to take into account. Therefore, practitioners may not be able to use the predictive value of a knowledge claim or theory such as "If X then Y. . ." but instead may find it a helpful heuristic to consider X and Y as categories for stimulating a new way of thinking about a practice or situation.[2] For example, learning style inventories attempt to identify and label types of learners and to explain why some people learn better from different instructional approaches than others. Although many teachers object to the notion that such inventories can be used to predict how students will respond to different kinds of learning activities, they find the concepts helpful in thinking about teaching strategies and planning lessons.

Although the products produced from any paradigm of research can be used in this way, interpretive research lends itself well to this analytical approach given its concern with identifying conceptual categories (rather than discrete variables or behaviors) of meaning and interaction that shape life in schools (Popkewitz, 1986). The purpose of this kind of research is to generate understandings and interpretations of the subjective meanings that people give to their actions and the rules that govern their social interactions. A central assumption is that actions or behaviors are inseparable from their actor's intentions, and, therefore, intent and purpose are seen as important for understanding educational actions and activities. Unlike empirical-analytic research, the parameters of knowledge are not predefined but grow out of individuals' sharing their interpretations of the world.

Research in this tradition "presumes that teaching is a highly complex, context-specific, interactive activity in which differences across classrooms, schools, and communities are critically important" (Cochran-Smith & Lytle, 1993, p. 6). So interpretive research attempts to illuminate the complex social realities of school life in a particular setting by providing a contextually rich description of patterns of actions in classrooms and schools and the meanings and interpretations that the teachers and other participants ascribe to them. The interpretive researcher usually analyzes and presents these patterns in conceptual terms and, thus, the product of qualitative research offers conceptual insights and frameworks that can assist readers to reflect on their own school lives. These patterns and concepts that are revealed in qualitative case studies differ from the lawlike relationships stated for the practitioner by empirical-analytical research and represent a different kind of generalization. The reader, rather than the researcher, is left to establish the transferability of any generalized understandings by drawing analogies to his or her own context (Wehlage, 1981). Engagement in this reasoning process can contribute to the practitioner's deliberations on his or her own work.

Practitioner Involvement in Knowledge Construction

Interpretive and empirical-analytic research is traditionally conducted within a knowledge creation, dissemination, and utilization model, and practitioners tend to be involved only in the utilization phase as consumers or implementers of the products of research (except, for example, when they are conducting research to meet the requirements for a graduate degree, collecting data for accountability purposes, or investigating a local school or district concern). In this model, the role of the educational researcher is viewed as a detached observer who makes all the decisions about the design of the study, the collection and analysis of data, and the conclusions to be drawn. The power and privilege to pose the questions to be studied, interpret information collected, and draw conclusions is generally in the hands of the researcher. In other words, this model does not recognize the local knowledge of practitioners in the research process, other than as subjects or informants, although in some qualitative or ethnographic research, practitioners may be involved in interpretation of information collected. Instead, the task of inquiring into and theorizing about educational practice is viewed as the responsibility of the researcher and not the practitioner.

Yet thoughtful practitioners also engage in a form of inquiry in making decisions about their practice. For example, teachers determine their objectives, consider a range of possible pedagogical actions for achieving those objectives, make a judgment about an appropriate course of action based on information available to them, observe the consequences of their actions, analyze and make inferences about those observations, and then modify their subsequent actions or store that information for future reference. Furthermore, research on teacher thinking has indicated "that teachers develop and hold implicit theories about their students, about the subject matter they teach and about their roles and responsibilities and how they should act" (Clark, 1986, cited in Eraut, 1994, p. 72). Stated another way, educational practitioners are constantly involved in interpreting their world and "theorizing,"[3] albeit usually implicitly, about their intentions and actions. In fact, both practitioners and social scientists are engaged in drawing inferences and making judgments based upon their interpretations of social reality (Codd, 1989). There is a difference, however, in how each group carries out this task. Concepts and ideas for interpreting practice can be derived from either discipline-based theory or from reflection on experience (Eraut, 1994). Social scientists explicitly and predominantly use public theory (but also draw on personal or experiential knowledge), whereas most practitioners tend to rely on their personal, often implicit theories (but also use some disciplinary knowledge).

Research as Co-Constructing
Ways of Viewing Practice

Research can involve a more interactive and reciprocal relationship in which practitioners contribute to the construction and reconstruction of knowledge by, for example, being encouraged to explicate their theories of practice and to comment on and react to empirical information and ideas presented to them. Teachers and administrators may also communicate problems and concerns that become questions included in research, be involved in data collection, and be critics of preliminary interpretations and conclusions. Put simply, this approach treats practitioners as more equal partners in research by acknowledging their expertise and local, contextualized knowledge of the practices being studied. However, in contrast to the subsequent approach to be discussed, the research agenda remains in the control of researchers, and the practitioners who are research subjects are not as viewed as independent inquirers or generators of theoretical or propositional knowledge.

An example of this approach is the work of the Professional Development Network (PDN), which was established within the Graduate School of Education (GSE) at the State University of New York at Buffalo (UB) in 1994. The purpose of this network is to connect local "individuals and groups in ways that enable them to work together more productively toward mutual goals" by furthering "the research-policy-practice linkages essential for substantive educational reform" (C. Cornbleth, personal communication, April, 1994). Research projects supported by PDN are grounded in local knowledge of the school setting, its prevailing practices, and educational change, as well as ways of bringing this knowledge to bear on specific questions or tasks. The contribution of insiders is intended to provide this grounding and joint planning, contribute resources to support the project, and allow for possible expansion and eventual institutionalization. All projects are required to demonstrate actual or potential benefit to the school or community.

The goals of a major policy-practice research project supported by this network are to study, critique, and enhance curriculum, instruction, and assessment efforts associated with a statewide reform effort, with a focus on the areas of social studies, English-language arts, and math-science-technology. University researchers involved in this project are exploring with school participants interpretations of the new state curriculum standards and issues of mutual concern that emerge from these policy statements. University project members try to respond to questions of interest and to contribute to ongoing reform through monitoring and documentation, evaluation, and feedback to participating schools. For example, data collected by one school to try to understand their faculty's perceptions of students were coded and categorized by a researcher working in the school. In this case, teachers and administrators had identified a broad empirical question of interest and had collected data to address that question, but lacked the time and expertise to analyze the data. After the data was organized into a more manageable and meaningful form, the researcher met with school faculty to discuss the meaningfulness of the categories that he had created and interpretations of the data and conclusions that might be drawn, including how this information might be used by the school.

This case highlighted a need to extend the work of PDN to include university faculty support for school-initiated research projects. So PDN is being replaced by a Collaborative Research Network that encourages teachers and administrators in local schools to become more involved in the study of research-policy-practice connections by inviting them to initiate ideas for collaborative research projects. The vehicle for such an invitation is the use of small-scale Requests for Proposals (RFPs). Through these RFPs we hope to involve local educators in collaborative projects right from the beginning stages of the research process and to establish relationships and conditions that are more likely to lead to their development of a sense of ownership of and commitment to substantive school-based reform efforts.

The conception of knowledge underlying this co-construction of understanding of practice is similar to that described previously in using research findings as analytical constructs, but in this case practitioners are actively involved in contributing to the construction of the research "findings." Knowledge "use," however, begins during the research process, such that knowledge production and dissemination are not treated as separate and dichotomous functions—at least not for the practitioners working in the school setting in which the research takes place. Practitioners contribute their experiential knowledge (i.e., concepts and ideas derived from experience or personal practice) to the researchers' discipline-based knowledge (i.e., systems of ideas in the public domain derived from systematic inquiry), and new understandings and meanings are constructed. This process of attempting to develop a deeper understanding by integrating different perspectives and ways of knowing requires that both parties explicate the knowledge they bring to the situation. The process of theorizing that takes place should involve both putting public theories into use by giving them contextually specific meaning and reviewing private theories already in use (Eraut, 1994). However, given that public theories tend to be viewed as the province of university researchers and practical theories the domain of practitioners, the researcher is likely to focus on the articulation and reconstruction of empirical propositions or conceptual insights and explanations, whereas the practitioners are likely to be predominantly concerned with rethinking practical actions based on new empirical data or conceptual ideas. Therefore, this co-construction of the reality of practice "creates a means for communication between researchers and practitioners, but does not intend to alter the fundamental relationships between them" (Noffke, 1996, p. 306).

Nevertheless, the practitioner's experience in co-constructing knowledge can lead to a different perception of and approach to the use of research.

Research as an Integral Part of Practice

In co-constructing an understanding of practice, the research agenda and process remains in the control of researchers studying other people's practices. Usually these researchers are external to the school, but they can be practitioners who are conducting research outside their own classroom or office. Teachers and administrators may have some input into someone else's research project by contributing to parts of the research process (as described in the last approach), but research is not an ongoing part of their practice. In other words, educational practice is seen as a separate activity from educational research. Practitioners are recognized as possessing local personalized knowledge but are not often seen as capable of generating formal or theoretical knowledge that is usually treated as the desired end. Furthermore, knowledge remains viewed as a commodity that is created by some people and used by others; thus knowledge remains separated from action.

In contrast, research can be conducted by practitioners within the context of their everyday work life. This kind of research is concerned with addressing educators' immediate knowledge—and action—needs for the purposes of improving practice or enhancing understanding of practice (Richardson, 1994). In other words, practitioner research tends to be used in the same setting in which it is conducted and is usually oriented toward taking actions that address a particular concern or situation. Consequently, this type of research is commonly referred to as action research.[4] The focus can be on individual, group, or schoolwide practices, and the work can be conducted by an individual or a group within the school, or in conjunction with outside collaborators.

Although having a relatively long (and checkered) history, dating back over 50 years, only in recent years has action research received significant attention in both academic and school circles. Accompanying this attention, however, there has been a proliferation in the variety of uses of the term. In some versions, action research is conceptualized in a way that offers few challenges to traditional research, but in others it is seen as representing a new paradigm (Carr & Kemmis, 1983; Cochran-Smith & Lytle, 1993; Stevenson, 1995; Winter, 1989). In the former case, the focus is on solving local problems by following the usual procedures of traditional research but on a sufficiently small scale for practitioners to use.

The concern here, however, is with forms of action research that emphasize the value of subjective and experiential knowing in which practitioners construct and use their own knowledge of practice from inquiry that is grounded in practice. The action research process is built upon the existing propensity and commitment of most practitioners to study and to improve their work but provides a more systematic, more rigorous,[5] and more collaborative means of doing so. A common methodology involves a spiral of recursive cycles of planning, acting, observing, and reflecting to address a particular concern or situation. But instead of collecting data in order to decide what actions to take, "the action researcher is studying the intentions, consequences and circumstances of actions she or he has taken, as well as using the information to influence further actions" (Stevenson, 1995, p. 200). Thus, unlike traditional academic research that "frowns on intervening in any way in the research setting, action research demands some form of intervention" (Anderson, Herr, & Nihlen, 1994, p. 12). This intervention, as part of an action cycle, is intended to increase the practitioner-researcher's knowledge of his or her original question or concern, which in turn should lead to a subsequent and improved intervention or educational action. Knowledge construction and utilization, therefore, alternate as practice informs theory and theory informs practice.

Although practitioner-researchers possess a wealth of local knowledge from working daily in their research context, much of this knowledge is tacit. Part of the action research process is to subject one's theories (beliefs, assumptions, values, commitments) and practices to critical scrutiny—by oneself and others. This requires articulating the intentions and rationales underlying one's educational actions; reflecting on one's actions; and critically examining the relationships among intentions, circumstances, actions, and consequences (McTaggart, 1992). Different perspectives should be obtained from "critical friends" or collaborators, and different sources of data should be collected to discipline, not remove, subjectivity and to challenge inappropriate analyses. Public theories (and the concepts and ideas from them) also have a role to play by providing an alternative frame for reinterpreting experience and by enlarging one's vision by directing attention to important aspects that otherwise might go unnoticed (Prawat, 1991). The purpose is for practitioners to engage with their own actions and with others in a critically self-reflective way so as to enhance their understanding of their practice and its underlying theories. The understanding and improvement of practice through action research is grounded in an epistemology of action and an experiential way of knowing: that knowledge arises in and for action (Reason, 1994), but the appropriate methods of validating such knowledge claims remain somewhat unclear and are the subject of current debate (Stevenson, 1995; Winter, 1989).

Implications for the Preparation
of Teachers and School Administrators

Traditionally, most teacher education and administrative preparation programs are based on two central assumptions: (a) that knowledge is first acquired and then later, when deemed appropriate, used; and (b) that knowledge of most worth is derived from discipline-based inquiry. As a result of these assumptions, the primary focus of such programs has been on the acquisition of social science theory with very little attention given to the use of theory. Yet all students enter preparation programs with their own assumptions, beliefs, and values regarding educational theory, research, and practice. Commonly, for example, students entering programs at the UB seem to believe that theory is constructed only by philosophers and researchers; research is a complex activity requiring sophisticated statistical analysis of quantitative data that is conducted only by people in universities; and good educational practice involves applying knowledge generated by the best research. The ideas that theory and research are socially constructed and educational practice is problematic are rarely part of students' initial belief systems.

The assumptions and beliefs about educational theory and practice held by students are frequently excluded as a subject of discussion in preparation programs. For example, the common student assumption that social science theory is to be applied directly to their later practice is rarely challenged by explicitly addressing other ways that theory and research can inform educational practice. Students then tend to dismiss research-generated theory as irrelevant when they find that it cannot be applied directly to their practice.

The assumptions underlying traditional preparation programs also conflict with the notion that not only does an idea get reinterpreted during use, "it also may need to be used before it acquires any significant meaning to the user" (Eraut, 1994, p. 81). Put simply, such programs tend to treat educators as people who practice but do not theorize (Zeichner & Liston, 1996). But, as previously stated, theories and ideas derived from research are important for providing educators with an extended array of concepts for questioning and theorizing about what they are doing. Social science theory also is important for enabling students to place teaching and schooling within an institutional and societal context (Zeichner & Liston, 1987). Therefore, instead of leaving students entirely dependent on their own devices to integrate new concepts and ideas into their existing frameworks, preparation programs should expose students to theoretical and research-based ideas and frameworks for understanding and interpreting practice in the context of explicating their own espoused theories. Public theories can provide both a language and source of new ideas for articulating and clarifying one's practical theories, as well as a source for critiquing existing beliefs and understandings. Some programs, for example, use reflective writing in the form of student journals (Oberg, 1990) and/or educational platforms (Osterman & Kottkamp, 1993) to encourage students to articulate their own beliefs (e.g., about teaching and learning, education and schooling, students and subject matter), as well as their values and commitments. Selected theoretical works and reflection on practical experiences, such as school observations and practice teaching or internships, are used to help students analyze and question their beliefs in more depth and subsequently revise them in light of new understandings.

Inquiry-oriented preparation programs usually do not adopt the traditional premise about the acquisition and use of theory. Rather than viewing educators as passive recipients and implementers of knowledge created in universities, they are cast as active agents who need to make complex judgments based on critically reflective inquiry into their own experiences and situation. These programs, therefore, tend to emphasize the use of research texts—not as prescriptive guidelines for practice, but as vehicles for thinking about and analyzing practice. Many programs involve practitioners as well as university faculty as instructors or co-instructors in order to enable students to draw on different experiences and perspectives in constructing their understandings of practice.

The curriculum for the Leadership Initiative for Tomorrow's Schools (LIFTS) program at UB (see Chapter 4), instead of comprising discipline-based courses, is structured around inquiries into issues and dilemmas of practice being encountered in schools. These inquiries draw upon both disciplinary and experiential knowledge as needed to further understanding of the particular issue being studied. The intent is to use theory to inform practice and practice to inform theory, based on the assumption of a reciprocal relationship. For example, the program's second cohort (for which I was the coordinating instructor) spent the greater part of a semester addressing the question, What does authentic teaching look like and how can it be encouraged? We began to examine this question by sharing among cohort members the experiences, knowledge, and values that were embedded in our own teaching in an effort to tentatively articulate our personal, practical theories of authentic teaching. Then we turned to investigating external knowledge by researching and reading relevant literature and by engaging in intensive discussions with various resource people. Here the conceptual and empirical work of researchers at the Center on Organization and Restructuring of Schools on authentic instruction was found to be particularly compelling for informing our understandings (Newmann, Secada, & Wehlage, 1995; Newmann & Wehlage, 1995). Students, however, spent considerable time, both individually and collectively, making their own sense of the rubrics developed by these researchers for determining the intellectual quality and authenticity standards of assessment tasks, instruction, and student performance. In debating the meanings and interpretations of this work, students were likely influenced by their own biographies and work experiences as well as by their experiences in the program and my own personal familiarity with the history of the ideas informing this research. Thus, according to Handal and Per Lauvas (1987), each student's understanding was dependent on an integration of personal and programmatic experiences, received knowledge, and central values. Observations also were conducted in local schools to try to make abstract concepts and principles reflexive with the conditions of classroom work and to create a common experience for further exploring our understandings of authentic instruction. In short, students and instructors attempted to co-construct an understanding of the issue that was grounded both in the study of practice and the study of scholarship, as well as in each individual's educational values and commitments.

Students in both administrative preparation and teacher education also should have the opportunity to develop the knowledge, skills, and dispositions for conducting research as an integral part of professional practice. To this end, action research was introduced by the author as an elective graduate course in 1989 at UB as part of inservice teacher education and preservice administrator preparation programs (Stevenson, 1991). This course engages practitioner-students in conducting action research cycles of planning and enacting ideas for improving their own practice, observing and reflecting on the effects of their actions, and then (on the basis of those reflections) planning revised actions and thus continuing the cycle. More recently, as Emihovich describes in Chapter 3, action research has also become a part of the preservice teacher education program at UB.

In summary, preparation programs should expand students' conceptions of sources and types of knowledge about teaching and schooling; encourage them to articulate and critique their own (usually tacit) understandings, beliefs, and values about teaching and schooling; emphasize the problematic nature of knowledge of educational practice; give attention to the acquisition and use of academic/public concepts and theories for expanding students' capacity to understand and interpret educational practice; and, finally, develop students' understanding of and capacity to use action (or similar forms of) research for engaging in systematic inquiry into and reflection on their own practice.

Implications for the Role of University Researchers

Even some researchers who subscribe to the view that research findings can provide guidelines for practice believe it is not their responsibility to explicitly identify guidelines that might flow from their own studies, leaving it to practitioners to make the necessary inferences for practice from the findings presented. Other researchers, however, offer specific suggestions for educators that they believe emerge from their research findings. Some university faculty also contribute to furthering the use of new knowledge to improve practice by synthesizing research findings and working with schools to help translate them into practical actions, especially in relation to the application of complex techniques. Even if the production of new knowledge remains "my work," the application of that knowledge to improved practice should become viewed as "our work" by university and school faculty (see Chapter 2). As publicly supported workers, it can be argued that educational researchers have an obligation to establish the relevance of their work; therefore, every research report should explicitly indicate the ways in which inferences drawn from it might apply to practice (McTaggart, 1992). The role and responsibilities of university researchers, however, do not end there.

Researchers need to self-critically examine their own work in terms of its contribution to the common good and be able to justify the significance of systematic inquiry in general and their scholarship in particular for improving educational theory and practice, particularly at a time in which the role of universities and educational research is subject to increased public scrutiny and skepticism. Although this skepticism might be simply attributed to a broad dissatisfaction with the performance of public institutions (including universities and schools), the increasing complexity of postmodern society and resultant uncertainty about the solution of social and economic problems is probably also an important factor. During the past couple of decades the nature of research has been undergoing similar dramatic changes to family structures, the economy, technology, and access to information. For example, ways of viewing and understanding the world have changed to the extent that social science inquiry is no longer dominated by a single set of methodologies borrowed from the natural sciences; today, a diverse array of research methodologies is commonly employed. Part of this proliferation of methodologies is due to a postmodern loss of faith in objectivity and a recognition of diverse ways of experiencing and knowing the world. But this pluralism also has created a significant level of confusion and ambiguity about the value of research among practitioners and the public. The knowledge explosion and the emergence of cultural relativism threaten to devalue all systematic forms of inquiry (Schratz & Walker, 1995). The former has rendered the notion of simply collecting information a trivial task, whereas the latter reduces validated knowledge to an entirely individual construction—a proposition that poses grave consequences for efforts to create more communal and democratic forms of living.

The quality of educational practice is dependent in part on the quality of educators' reflective thought about their practice, and sustained inquiry can contribute to the depth and insight of such thought. Although educational practice is primarily concerned with "doing something rather than knowing something, . . . the doing is best accomplished in the presence of knowing" (Short, 1991, p. 11). In other words, the more trustworthy the state of knowing in which practitioners make decisions about appropriate actions, the better informed those actions are likely to be. Consequently, educational actions should be consistently informed by reliable knowledge generated by systematic inquiry. The quality of such inquiry is dependent on the expertise with which it is conducted, as well as the conditions in which it is conducted. It is this expertise, and specialized formal knowledge, that university researchers bring to both traditional and collaborative inquiry.

Researchers, however, also need to keep in mind that research knowledge is just one source of information that policymakers and practitioners consider in shaping educational policy or practice, a situation that has been highlighted by the politicization of education and schooling (and research). Many other influences act on educational policy and practice, as Glass (1987) makes clear:

Facts, even when accumulated into "research findings," seldom compel policies or political actions. Generally, findings are fragmentary or incomplete or, taken en masse, too incoherent to serve as justification for certain serious actions. Consider an example: When the judge in the Los Angeles desegregation case was confidently informed by sociologists that busing between the San Fernando Valley and downtown Los Angeles would result in the flight of 33% of the Anglo families from the public school system, he merely redrew the busing patterns so that the numbers of Anglos, Blacks, and Hispanics would balance after a third of the Anglos had fled the system. Policies grow out of "world views" and projections of possible futures, and these depend on many more things than research findings. (p. 9)

Two partnerships between the University of Illinois–Chicago and the K–12 school community in Chicago illustrate such issues, as well as the challenges and opportunities for university faculty to collaborate with schools (Braskamp & Wergin, 1996). The first project, "The Nation of Tomorrow" (TNT), was intended to "develop communities of support and to use the school as a developmental center" (p. 6). The second partnership, which was initiated by the Illinois Legislature, directly involved Chicago area universities in school reform by asking them to provide training for local school council members. A coalition of universities, the Chicago Public Schools, and other educational and community organizations was organized to plan and implement the training. These partnerships, according to Braskamp and Wergin (1996), revealed that faculty "are not accustomed to the messiness of direct engagement in societal problems" (p. 9), such as wrestling with partisan struggles over seeking closure (nonuniversity participants) or continuing study and debate (university participants); have limited experiential knowledge of schools and reform, to the extent that "their analyses often seemed to look like naive textbook answers to those in the fray" (p. 9); were confronted with questions that do not lend themselves to traditional research approaches and lacked expertise in conducting research over which one has little control; and needed "a different set of conceptual, social and professional skills" (p. 11) to that demanded by traditional scholarship.

On the other hand, once trust and commitment had been built among all parties, new forms of faculty scholarship emerged that influenced the collaborative work of the partners.

What faculty often lacked in experiential knowledge and hands on involvement with training local citizens, they made up in their experience in pedagogy and knowledge of educational reform in general. Faculty were more able to think "out of the box" because they did not feel compelled to defend past practices, were more intellectually self-confident (maybe even arrogant at times), more skilled at writing and interpreting concepts and information into a theoretical context. Thus, the differing perspectives became reinforcing and complementary once mutual trust existed. (Braskamp & Wergin, 1996, p. 16)

Braskamp and Wergin (1996) argue that in the past the university has assumed and communicated to the public a view that it possesses a higher order of truth that can help provide solutions to the problems of our society. As a result of the partnership experiences at the University of Illinois–Chicago, some faculty and administrators now acknowledge that they can serve society better by taking joint responsibility with local schools for educational reform and participating "in a community of truth makers always searching for but never finding ultimate truths" (p. 21).

Conclusion

Embedded in traditional views of research are a number of dichotomies—about theory and practice, knowledge and action, facts and values, objectivity and subjectivity—that are based on a technical rationality or instrumental worldview. These distinctions have begun to blur with the advent of other forms of rationality and ways of knowing to the extent, I would argue, that each of these dichotomies is an example of what the sociologist George Homans terms a "false dichotomy." These newer epistemologies are based on a belief that "truth" cannot be separated from personal experiences (Braskamp & Wergin, 1996). Therefore, there is also a need to rethink the role of the researcher and his or her relationship with the researched "subject" given that their respective roles and identities can no longer be as easily demarcated.

As a start, we can treat research, action, and learning as interwoven parts of a process in which participation is a prerequisite (Schratz & Walker, 1995). Those who conduct original empirical research might contribute to the improvement of educational practice, and in turn improve their educational research, by entering into a dialogue with practitioners on the meaning, including the moral purposes, and utility of their work. This dialogue should not wait until research findings are in hand; it should begin with a negotiation with practitioners of the kinds of questions that need to be addressed in their particular setting, and it should continue by recognizing the knowledge and expertise that is embedded in their practice. Such a dialogue would provide a beginning to the creation of a more democratic research process and one that ultimately is more likely to contribute to the improvement of educational practice.

Notes

1. I am indebted to Stephen Brown for this point.
2. I am also indebted to Stephen Brown for this point.

3. I define *theorize,* not in conventional terms of meaning to develop a theory, but "to interpret, explain, or judge intentions, actions, and experiences" (Eraut, 1994, p. 71).

4. *Teacher research/inquiry, action science inquiry, participatory (action) research, practical inquiry* and *practitioner research/inquiry* are also some of the labels used to describe the same or a similar type of research activity. Many, however, are unwilling to use the term *research* because the primary purpose, they argue, is not to produce generalizations or expand the general knowledge base (Richardson, 1994), although others argue that both the products, in terms of findings and raw data, and the process of theorizing can contribute to the knowledge base on teaching (Elliott, 1977-1978).

5. The conception of *rigor* in action research differs from positivistic or interpretivist research and is not derived from particular techniques of collecting or analyzing data. Instead, according to some writers, rigor is derived from the coherence of justifications of proposed actions and from the coherence of interpretations of observations and reflections of the consequences and circumstances of actions (Carr & Kemmis, 1983).

References

Anderson, G. L., Herr, K., & Nihlen, A. S. (1994). *Studying your own school: An educator's guide to qualitative practitioner research*. Thousand Oaks, CA: Corwin.

Borg, W., & Gall, M. (1991). *Educational research: An introduction* (5th ed.). New York: Longman.

Braskamp, L. A., & Wergin, J. F. (1996). Forming new social partnerships. In W. G. Tierney (Ed.), *The responsive university: Restructuring for high performance*. Baltimore: John Hopkins University Press.

Carr, W., & Kemmis, S. (1983). *Becoming critical: Knowing through action research*. Geelong, Victoria: Deakin University Press.

Cochran-Smith, M., & Lytle, S. (1993). *Inside/outside: Teacher research and knowledge*. New York: Teachers College Press.

Codd, J. (1989). Educational leadership as reflective action. In J. Smyth (Ed.), *Critical perspectives on educational leadership* (pp. 157-178). London: Falmer.

Doyle, W. (1987). Research on teaching effects as a resource for improving instruction. In M. Wideen & Andrews (Eds.), *Staff development for school improvement* (pp. 91-102). New York: Falmer.

Driscoll, A., & Stevens, D. (1985). *Classroom teachers' response to the research on effective instruction.* Paper presented at the annual meeting of the American Educational Research Association, Chicago.

Elliott, J. (1977-1978). Developing hypotheses about classrooms from teachers' practical constructs: An account of the work of the Ford Teaching Project. *Interchange, 7*(2), 2-22.

Eraut, M. (1994). The acquisition and use of educational theory by beginning teachers. In G. R. Harvard & P. Hodkinson (Eds.), *Action and reflection in teacher education.* Norwood, NJ: Ablex.

Glass, G. (1987). What works: Politics and research. *Educational Researcher, 16*(3), 5-10.

Green, J., & Chandler, S. (1990). Toward a dialog about implementation within a conceptual cycle of inquiry. In E. G. Guba (Ed.), *The paradigm dialog* (pp. 202-215). Newbury Park, CA: Sage.

Handal, G., & Per Lauvas, P. (1987). *Promoting reflective teaching.* Milton Keynes, UK: Open University Press.

Hirst, P. (1979). Professional studies in initial teacher education: Some conceptual issues. In R. Alexander & E. Wormald (Eds.), *Professional studies for teaching.* Guildford, UK: Society for Research in Higher Education.

Huberman, M. (1983). Recipes for busy kitchens: A situational analysis of routine knowledge use in schools. *Knowledge: Creation, Diffusion, Utilization, 4*(4), 478-510.

Kagan, D. (1990). Ways of evaluating teacher cognition: Inferences concerning the Goldilocks principle. *Review of Educational Research, 60*(3), 419-469.

Kennedy, M. (1984). How evidence alters understanding and decisions. *Educational Evaluation and Policy Analysis, 6*(3), 207-226.

McIntyre, D. (1980). The contributions of research to quality in teacher education. In E. Hoyle & J. Megarry (Eds.), *Professional development of teachers* (pp. 293-307). London: Kogan Page.

McTaggart, R. (1992). Appraising reports of inquiry. In D. Caulley, H. Moore, & J. Orton (Eds.), *Social science methodology for educational inquiry: A conceptual overview.* Beijing: Beijing Teachers College Press.

Newmann, F., Secada, W., & Wehlage, G. (1995). *A guide to authentic instruction and assessment: Vision, standards and scoring.* Madison: Wisconsin Center for Education Research.

Newmann, F., & Wehlage, G. (1995). *Successful school restructuring.* Madison: Wisconsin Center for Education Research.

Noffke, S. (1996). Professional, personal and political dimensions of action research. *Review of Educational Research, 22,* 305-343.

Oberg, A. (1990). Methods and meanings in action research: The action research journal. *Theory into Practice, 29*(3), 214-221.

Osterman, K., & Kottkamp, R. (1993). *Reflective practice for educators: Improving schooling through professional development.* Newbury Park, CA: Corwin.

Popkewitz, T. (1986). Paradigm and purpose. In C. Cornbleth (Ed.), *An invitation to research in social education* (pp. 10-27). Washington, DC: National Council for the Social Studies.

Prawat, R. (1991). Conversations with self and settings: A framework for thinking about teacher empowerment. *American Educational Research Journal, 28*(4), 737-757.

Reason, P. (1994). Three approaches to participative inquiry. In N. Denzin & Y. Lincoln (Eds.), *Handbook of qualitative research* (pp. 324-339). Thousand Oaks, CA: Sage.

Richardson, V. (1994). Conducting research on practice. *Educational Researcher, 23*(5), 5-10.

Schratz, M., & Walker, R. (1995). *Research as social change: New opportunities for qualitative research.* London: Routledge.

Short, E. (1991). Introduction: Understanding curriculum inquiry. In E. Short (Ed.), *Forms of curriculum inquiry* (pp. 1-25). Albany: State University of New York Press.

Stevenson, R. (1991). Action research as professional development: A U.S. case study of inquiry-oriented inservice education. *Journal of Education for Teaching, 17*(3), 277-292.

Stevenson, R. (1995). Action research and supportive school contexts: Exploring the possibilities for transformation. In S. Noffke & R. Stevenson (Eds.), *Educational action research: Becoming practically critical* (pp. 197-209). New York: Teachers College Press.

Stevenson, R. (1996). Knowledge-in-use: Reconceptualizing the use of knowledge in school decision making. In S. Jacobson, E. Hickcox & R. Stevenson (Eds.), *School administration: Persistent dilemmas in preparation and practice* (pp. 247-255) Westport, CT: Praeger.

Tom, A. (1980). The reform of teacher education through research: A futile quest. *Teachers College Record, 82*(1), 15-29.

Toomey, R. (1977). Teachers' approaches to curriculum planning: An exploratory study. *Curriculum Inquiry, 7*(2), 121-129.

Wehlage, G. (1981). The purpose of generalization in field study research. In T. Popkewitz & R. Tabachnik (Eds.), *The study of schooling: Field based methodologies in educational research and evaluation* (pp. 211-226). New York: Praeger.

Winter, R. (1989). *Learning from experience: Principles and practice in action research*. London: Falmer.

Zeichner, K., & Liston, D. (1996). *Reflective teaching: An introduction*. Mahwah, NJ: Lawrence Erlbaum.

Zeichner, K., & Liston, D. (1987). Teaching student teachers to reflect. *Harvard Educational Review, 57*(1), 23-48.

6

Where Are We Going?

Stephen L. Jacobson, Catherine Emihovich,
Jack Helfrich, Hugh G. Petrie, and
Robert B. Stevenson

This final chapter reports a conversation held on December 18, 1996, that involved all five of the book's authors. The week before, we had shared draft versions of our chapters with one another and then used this discussion to examine the central themes that had emerged from our work. We felt that we had a unique opportunity to use this conversation to inform activities we were currently engaged in at the Graduate School of Education (GSE) at the State University of New York at Buffalo (UB).

After each of us summarized what we felt were the key elements of our respective chapters, we spent the next 90 minutes addressing the central question of this book: How should we prepare educators for tomorrow's schools in tomorrow's schools of education? And, more specifically, with regard to our own work lives, what are the implications of these chapters for greater collaboration in educator preparation at UB's Graduate School of Education?

Although the five of us have been involved in numerous change initiatives and collaborations over the years, it is rare that we have had the time to simply reflect as a group upon where we see ourselves heading as an institution and what impediments we anticipate. Typically, the last chapter of a text such as this one would be reserved for the senior editor or lead author to offer some concluding remarks. We decided instead to try something different. Because this is a book about change, collaboration, and new ways of doing things, Hugh Petrie proposed that we end the book with a conversation among ourselves. We saw this as a wonderful opportunity to do something we felt we needed to do anyway, so we jumped at the chance. What follows is the edited text of that conversation, presented almost verbatim, with occasional commentary to introduce and consider major themes as they emerged. These themes included changing conceptions of leadership, resistance to change, the implications of chaos theory and organizational stability, the moral dimensions of leadership, and the need for a trust-building process that would foster long-term commitment.

Our conversation begins with Jacobson noting that in a number of chapters, particularly Emihovich's and his own, it is suggested that teacher and administrator preparation be drawn into a closer working relationship. The obvious question this new relationship poses is whether such an integration is possible and, if so, how that might be accomplished. Very quickly, programmatic issues of time constraint and differences in the appropriate purpose and focus of the two programs surface among the discussants.

Jacobson: I can see overlaps in the preparation of teachers and administrators, particularly if we focus on leadership. But as Catherine's chapter makes clear, there is already so much work faced by preservice teachers that it is hard to imagine how we could add more. This attitude seems typical of many of our specialized programs. In traditional administrative preparation, for example, the assumption is that students already know about teaching and learning since almost all are teachers. We don't feel we have enough time to go back over those issues so, at best, we require a course or two. We feel that we have to simply get on to the business of management and move in that direction. We feel pressed, and there is really no time or way to add additional pieces.

Stevenson: I guess I see those as two different issues. I have some concerns about pushing leadership into teacher education. Whether you view it as an add-on or integrated into the program, I'm not sure that we're really doing a good job as it is in preparation programs. Let's take teacher education. Where I think the focus should be is on helping prospective teachers to think pedagogically. There are so many different areas of study to include, and you have only 1 year to study them. Obviously, there is not enough time to work with people in a year. However, if we view the preparation of teachers as an ongoing activity, rather than just a year, we can address leadership during teachers' beginning years in the profession. I think we've got to maintain a focus in both programs. I think we need to focus on thoughtful pedagogy in the preparation of both teachers and administrators, and it worries me that if we start pushing leadership in the teacher education program, we're going to lose some of that focus, just like we lost the focus on teaching and learning in educational administration in the United States in recent decades by focusing on management.

Emihovich: Bob, I don't disagree with the point you're making, but what is helping me to think about this is not leadership qua leadership, but rather what I got out of Jack's chapter and what I see evident in some of the things happening with students. We try to build field teams where we place a large number of students into the same school to work with a group of teachers. Yet it's surprising how little attention we pay to group process and how people work together. Now *that* is a critical component of leadership—one that we don't usually think of as leadership. I think that's where we could begin to do a lot more, not so much with providing new skills but, rather, how to work together in groups. Even in my own classes where we do a lot of group work discussing case studies, students find it very difficult to reach consensus about ways of dealing with a particular case. What I see over and over again is students hanging on to their individual ways of dealing with things—just as they would as classroom teachers—rather than asking how to approach a situation collaboratively, which was what they would do as a team. I think we can provide more experiences, even within the current curriculum, that would allow them to work as teams both in class and on-site. I think this is an absolutely essential addition to teacher education.

Emihovich's notion of using group process skills as the component of leadership that might crosscut both teacher and administration preparation opens the conversation to an exploration of the utility of group facilitation at both the university and in the field. What follows is a series of personal reflections on differences in university and school district cultures with regard to group process. There emerge several key issues that appear to impede change initiatives: overcoming traditional perceptions of leadership, the lack of a shared vision (especially at the university), and perceived threats to professional autonomy and power. It is interesting to note disparities in the authors' perceptions of the relative autonomy of teachers and university faculty. These differences in opinion led the conversation to a consideration of the dynamic tension that exists between top-down and participatory approaches to facilitating change, and the general tendency to dichotomize key issues that surround change.

Petrie: I want to keep focused on this notion of process for a while because I think that is one of the issues that I found lurking in several of our chapters, explicitly in Jack's. I believe that process skills are very important. Yet our inability to utilize them in the university is significant. For example, we tried some planning last year that was not everything it should have been. The process was okay for some period, but it didn't go as far as it should have. There seems to be, in my judgment, a kind of built-in suspicion of process skills, especially at the university. Somehow this is seen as something that is too touchy-feely, and many people feel that it doesn't get down to the real substance or the real decisions. I found in trying to institute more process within GSE, and in arguing for more process within the larger university, that process is at best ignored and at worst denigrated. What can we do about that? Jack, was process ever seen as being "soft" in your district?

Helfrich: Initially, some board members felt that all you had to do was tell the staff what to do and they would do it. They thought, "You're the superintendent, just go ahead and tell them!" We have had about 150 years of experience with telling people what to do in schools and it never worked very well, but no one seems to realize it. Having lived through the process, I know that to make it work takes a lot of staying power and a lot of training, whether in a school, a school system, or school of education. You can't say "Just do it" because that doesn't work. There are stages of development you must go through in terms of a willingness to become involved in the process, learning leadership skills, and being willing to take on a leadership role. How do you get children involved in situations where they are encouraged to become leaders? If it starts in kindergarten, then leadership, as it matriculates through undergraduate and graduate school, isn't only something you teach; rather, it is something that you facilitate and support. Taking on leadership responsibility should be something we learn to do and something we learn to accept as individuals. Unfortunately, it is something we usually inhibit in schools, because most administrators are managers, not leaders. If you just tell somebody what to do and then back out of the process yourself, you aren't a leader.

Jacobson: I think this issue may be more difficult for a school of education than for a school district. You can ask people in a school district what their common purpose is and I think they would probably offer some consensus, a reasonably shared conception. I don't think we even come close to the kind of shared vision that might serve as a starting point here in the GSE.

Petrie: I believe in a way that the problem at the university is almost the exact opposite of the problem in schools. Jack, you were talking about schools having a culture of the leader telling you what to do. In contrast, the university has a culture in which we all, individually, know what to do, and so we're not going to let anyone else tell us what to do. Schools are used to being told what to do, while universities are used to nobody telling them what to do. Both approaches seem to lack the ability to find common ground. Maybe that's why process is so important. If we want to have simultaneous renewal in schools and schools of education but we're approaching it differently, then we have a problem.

Helfrich: I think the most common perception of leadership is that you simply tell people what to do. In fact, the reality of the situation is that the staff basically thinks, "We don't care what he says. We know what to do."

Emihovich: In that sense, Jack's right. I've long argued that the reason we don't see real change in schools is because it comes top-down. Teachers sit back, they go to workshops, they listen, they go back to their room, they close their door, and they do what they've always done or what they think should be done because they don't see the point of it. The bottom line is, except for the obligatory once-a-year evaluation visit from an administrator, in which you do your canned lesson, everybody is happy. You can get away with that forever. There is no one to call you to account. So Jack's absolutely right, that notion of autonomy is replicated at the classroom. But, on the other hand, we have more control at the university over our time, our schedule, and our teaching preferences. We have a lot more control than teachers.

Jacobson: I agree that we're cut more slack, but I'm not entirely sure that university faculty don't get in line and march in step once told what to do. We're often waiting to be told what to do.

Stevenson: I think that varies a lot.

Emihovich: I think it is a question of personality, but I do see some people waiting for direction.

Stevenson: But you are also likely to see fireworks when you get into telling faculty what to do without their input. I also wonder if another factor is involved here. That is, thinking in either/or terms. We either have top-down leadership or shared decision making. We either have a focus on substance or we have a focus on process. The concern about process is that we're going to lose the substance or content, but what we need is both. As Jack noted, there are situations which call for top-down leadership, yet everyone tends to dichotomize approaches— to think in either/or roles—and I see that tendency as entering the picture.

Stevenson's comments suggest that attempts to oversimplify complex issues by dichotomizing them may force colleagues into adversarial positions. The pressure to find the "one best solution" begs the need for a greater appreciation of the diverse ways in which people are influenced to change and the need to find an appropriate balance among seemingly competing viewpoints. As the conversation continues to unfold, we examine these influences on change and consider both the centrality of preparation experiences in shaping an individual's future practice and the need for new organizational structures to help reshape current leadership practices.

Emihovich: Some people argue that dichotomizing is a product of Western philosophy. We see things in binary or dichotomized categories, whereas other societies can see things simultaneously, therefore they don't have the same problem. I think Bob is right; there is a very strong mentality that dominates American culture that plays out as either we've got to do this or we've got to do that. We've got to find the single-best intervention, especially if we can just establish it by good, scientific research. Once you get that magic bullet, you can move. Instead of this "totalization" mentality, wherein things have to be all or nothing, maybe what we have to do is relax, sit back, and realize that the only thing I can change is myself. I can only really change my practice, I can't change yours.

Jacobson: But you can influence the practice of others.

Emihovich: Yes, in the process of me changing my practice, you might say, "That looks good, maybe I'll also try some of that." But you would have to make that choice.

Jacobson: I think there are critical points in one's development as an educator, such as during preparation, when these influences can be most profound. For example, if you don't see collaboration among faculty, or have a chance to collaborate with fellow students during your administrative preparation, how would you know how to collaborate in the field? How could you begin to reconceptualize traditional notions of leadership without the opportunity to be exposed to alternatives? While some faculty aren't threatened by changing notions of leadership, and welcome the opportunity to introduce them to our programs, I think others resist because it suggests that roles and relationships are going to have to change as well.

Helfrich: When it comes to the type of leadership we're discussing, I don't think we can talk about the majority of current administrators. In fact, I don't believe that "administration" per se is a viable concept anymore. Administrators, for the most part, have been taught to be managers who deal with the here and the now, whereas leaders ought to be dealing with the future. I think we need to be talking more about leadership. If schools are ever going to improve, we can't deal solely with problem solving, and that calls for a couple of conditions. The first condition is having parallel structures to deal with solving problems that occur every day. But that is not the same as looking toward the future and developing what needs to be done to make students successful. Thus, you've got to have both systems operating simultaneously.

A second condition that has to exist is focusing and follow-through. You must focus on things that will move you ahead and follow through in all kinds of ways to make sure that they happen. If you ask someone to draw a chart of how the schools are organized, it will probably be hierarchical in structure. They will say that the board of education is at the top, the superintendent directly below, and everything else falls below that point. Relationships that exist on the chart don't really exist. Schools are dynamic and chaotic, and never static. They are changing all the time. Somehow we've got to get that reality into the minds of leaders and of the people who will constitute the school community. The fact that they keep changing all the time requires we have structures in place that not only take advantage of change but support it.

Emihovich: I think Jack is raising a classic paradox; that is, schools are dynamic organizations in constant flux. But, at the same time, there are momentary points of stability around which people get things done. It is not an eternally changing place so that nothing gets done.

Helfrich: I didn't mean to imply that. However, trying to treat a dynamic organization as a static set of relationships does deter them from achieving many of the goals they set for themselves.

Emihovich: I knew that's what you meant. In the classic notion of chaos theory, random events can influence outcomes. There are periodic moments when a system stabilizes, then it gets disrupted, it changes, and then restabilizes at a different point. The trick is trying to get things done when you get those brief moments of stability, because sooner or later something is going to disrupt it again. So you're living with motion, while you're trying to get the work done.

The introduction of chaos theory into the conversation once again highlights the tension and complexity of change and resistance to change. Change is predicated on the existence of organizational stability, and stability can be perceived as being both beneficial and detrimental. The need for change, therefore, can be perceived simultaneously by faculty members as being detrimental and beneficial—resisted by those who view a current period of stability as productive in terms of their own needs, but supported by those seeking a new, more productive period of stability. This notion of change assumes that the actions of participants are intentional when, in fact, chaos theory suggests that sometimes changes are random occurrences, caused by factors outside the control of participants. When this is the case—that is, when change is the result of random, seemingly unrelated events—intentional change efforts may actually be attempts to resist random change, thus turning the earlier conception on its head. These apparent contradictions between change and stability are explored in the following interactions.

Petrie: We could have a good argument about chaos theory and whether it really has anything to say to education. However, the idea of moments of stability and moments of resistance are important, and those were themes that I found in virtually all of our discussions about people's attitude toward change. I view resistance to change as trying to maintain a kind of stability, and this is a kind of stability that we individually and collectively have to negotiate. However, all sorts of things, from random events to planned interventions, sometimes disrupt our accepted life, our work, or our view of life. Resistance to change is, in part, because these disturbances upset that equilibrium, and, in fact, most of our actions probably occur in an effort to maintain the existing stability, not to move to a new stability of some sort or another.

For example, many of our colleagues have a notion of what it means to be a professor—you can do your thing and I can do my thing—and they try to maintain that notion through an attitude of "live and let live." We each do our individual work. However, it is very important for people to understand what they really individually want. They may think they want one thing and focus on certain kinds of superficial issues, when what they really want is something else. If you can lead people to see that a change still allows them to get their deep needs satisfied, their deep values enacted, but in a slightly different kind of way, then maybe they have a chance of making some important changes and moving to a new node of stability. For example, collaborative work on designing an integrated preparation program for educators might better allow you, Steve, to pursue your individual research on leadership.

Stevenson: I'm glad that you introduced the notion of stability, because one of the things that worries me is a somewhat simplistic view of change and resistance to change. While there is a view that any resistance to change is negative, there is also a view that resistance to change can, in fact, be positive and actually help in weeding through proposals for change that aren't going to be beneficial. Another point you touched on, which I think is important, is that sometimes change is advocated or takes place in order to maintain continuity. Then resistance can create change. Stability and change are much more in tension than I think has been evident in the notion that all change is good.

The idea that resistance to change can sometimes be positive, because not all change initiatives are beneficial, quickly leads to an examination of moral leadership and the recognition of one's own voice in speaking out against injustice—other dimensions of leadership that must find a place in educator preparation. Examples are offered as to what these dimensions of leadership look like in practice and how they might be nurtured in preparation.

Emihovich: Right! Change isn't necessarily good. I think you're getting at another dimension we haven't discussed: the moral dimension of education. Some changes may have greater moral salience than others. Let me talk about that in context. We know that in many urban schools a large percentage of students are students of color. These schools are often deadening, alienating places. We have an entire generation of kids whose needs are not being met in public education. That is a resource this country can ill afford to lose given the demographic shifts in population. We are becoming a non-White society. We can't afford a situation that 50 to 100 years from now will result in a small elite, mostly White, running institutions peopled by large masses of non-Whites. I worry about what I hear from some of my students coming back from the city schools, saying what awful places these are for kids. Awful things are going on in schools. Teachers telling students openly, "You're stupid, you're never going to amount to anything, you're never going to succeed!" What does one do with that sensitive information? Do I have the authority to go into a class? I can drop some cooperating teachers, and I have, but do I have the authority to go to a teacher and say this is not right, you can't stand in front of a class and tell kids they're never going to amount to anything? How do we get students to talk about action research and keep reflecting on practice and changing practice when one of the practices happens to be something like that?

Stevenson: I think that comes back to something you referred to in Chapter 3: the importance of justifying your actions and not just focusing on your practices, but also looking at your intentions. There is also the issue of power relationships between student teachers and their supervising teachers in schools, which unfortunately creates a dynamic that makes it difficult for students to challenge them.

Jacobson: That's another aspect of leadership—recognition of one's voice. Leadership is speaking up to inspire others to challenge things that are wrong. It is something that has to be developed, and I guess you're suggesting that it sometimes gets suppressed.

Emihovich: Not sometimes. Their voices get suppressed all the time. I find it a horrible dilemma. I'm very distressed when my students come back and say a school is being run like a police state.

Petrie: Steve, you gave a marvelous example in Chapter 4 from the first year of LIFTS. The question was how the group would propose to solve the design issue of keeping existing teachers, mostly White, in the district, or hiring new ones, which might have led to a mix more closely resembling the district's racial makeup. And from your description, it appears that there was enough openness to allow the discussion to take place, although the cohort did approach it along racial lines.

Jacobson: It was tense. The group's first sympathies were with the teachers. How do we put teachers out on the street, whether Black or White? But then they began to ask, What are the implications for children in predominantly minority classrooms that have predominantly majority teachers? Would we be willing to hire a teacher of color who was not as strong a teacher as one who was White, in order to provide more role models in the classroom? When it was suggested that we might opt to let some good White teachers go in order to provide such a balance, it created considerable tension in the group along racial lines. But the group worked it out. Slowly, people begin to recognize where others were coming from on this issue. They began to understand life experiences they never before perceived, because they had developed enough trust in one another to engage in a dialogue.

Petrie: That was the question I was going to ask. What did that incident teach us about our preparation programs? I think what you're saying is we didn't resolve the racial issue, but we had in the preparation program just enough feeling of safety that people were willing to engage in the discussion even if they couldn't ultimately arrive at a consensus.

Jacobson: Yes, that was the intent. To provide a safe space for a discussion that was as tense as that one.

Emihovich: I had a case in my class last year where a student in the undergraduate class went out to do the action research piece, came back, and started to report about a neighborhood that was very poor and rundown. One of the African American students in the class said, "Excuse me, I know people who live in that area. They're not poor!" She really challenged it, and I was glad she felt she had the safety of a classroom to be able to do that. But we hear these remarks from students all the time, and my dilemma as an educator and what I model for my students is: How often do I call kids out on this? Where did you get that perception from? What do you mean by "this is a run-down neighborhood and all the households are poor"? These are hidden biases. I can stop that in my classroom, which I do, because I have the authority as a teacher and professor. But what happens when we carry it into a public school classroom? How do we get students to feel empowered to do it, and how do they do it? I don't know how to resolve this dilemma, and, as Hugh said, part of the problem is that I don't see us engaging in these kinds of conversations. Maybe we do it individually, and I'm sure some do, but there has to be a mechanism that raises this to a more sustained level. I think this is the role a university can play—that is, developing a moral dimension to leadership preparation by saying that we're not going to turn out people who don't raise these issues. Instead, we're going to turn out people who are going to make you feel uncomfortable, make you feel things are not so great in your district, because they ask tough questions such as: Who gets the money? Where do the resources go? How come resources are going here instead of there? Who made that decision? These are not comfortable questions.

By raising the specter of preparing students to ask uncomfortable questions, Emihovich's comments led the group back to considering the kinds of interactions between the university and the field that might typify new models of preparation. Specifically, there need to be frank, honest conversations about the appropriate role each should play—conversations that can only occur after considerable trust has been developed. The authors suggest that developing such a high level of trust will take time, commitment, a shift from organizational to community thinking, and mutual respect. Moreover, neither party should enter these discussions with either a fixed mind-set or a self-righteous attitude. Personal examples are offered about how trust was built within a school district, within our school of education, and across these institutions.

Petrie: One of the comments that Bob raised earlier had to do with the curriculum for teacher education, whether or not it was add-ons. One of the points made then was a very good one. Does one of the ways in which we collaborate consist of rethinking the roles that we in the university play in teacher and educator preparation and the roles that the schools themselves play in the preparation of educators? We've done some of that rethinking with the clinical faculty in teacher education and in the LIFTS program. However, the notion that the schools have, or might come to see themselves as having, a real role in this preparation is strikingly new for both constituencies. The idea would be that we don't have to do all of the preparation in higher education; some of it could be done later on in the schools. We would collaborate and figure out together what kind of teacher, leader, administrator, counselor we need and who could best do what part of the preparation.

I think that also suggests the issue that Catherine mentioned: How would we have the conversation with a school district where we might feel like saying, "You have some racist teachers in this school who are ruining the lives of these kids, and, at a minimum, we don't want to prepare our people here." That's an issue, and we would have to be able to have a safe conversation if we are really going to have collaborative efforts and simultaneous renewal. We would have to have safe conversations with our partners, just as we try to have safe conversations within our individual classes about some of these things. And that strikes me as another real tough conversation. I don't know how we begin to have those. Do I have the authority to say anything about the teachers in the classroom who appear to be doing really terrible things?

Emihovich: I did do that. We had a teacher who wasn't racist because she didn't discriminate; she told *all* the children they were stupid. She had low-achieving students, both Black and White, and she just told them, period, they were stupid. Our student teacher came back and reported this. I went to the principal and said, "I'm sorry, we have to pull the student out and we cannot use this teacher anymore and here's the reasons why." He knew she did it; everybody in the school knew she did it. The larger question is: How come they sanctioned that behavior?

Helfrich: Or ignored it.

Emihovich: But I did tell them we were pulling this student out and never giving this person another student again.

Jacobson: That's part of the shift from organizational to community thinking I propose in Chapter 4. In a community, if someone abuses neighborhood children, you do something about it. In an organization, we may not feel this is possible because of the potential ramifications. If we go to the district and we say we don't like what's happening, they may no longer provide us access. I think we have to stop thinking along organizational lines and start building community. But where do we begin? I don't know.

Stevenson: This is an example of self-interest, but the other concern here is that we need to be careful that we don't go in too often with our minds already made up and act in a self-righteous way. There are cases where we only have one perspective, and what we initially interpret as being, for example, racist might have another explanation. Now I'm not suggesting that is the case in the one Catherine just discussed. You probably took an extreme example, but in general I think we can't start with an attitude of moral superiority and certitude.

Helfrich: One of the things that came to mind when we were talking about these issues is the fact you need to build trust. When you're in a group where trust has been built, you can say pretty much what you want and it will be accepted, and you can respond in an open and honest manner, but that takes a long time. If you're talking about university-school collaboration, that's going to take even longer because you don't have the intimacy that you have within a school district. It's a different level of interaction, but I think it has to take place. I want to return to one of the things mentioned before about resource allocation. Who makes the decisions about where money goes? What we used to do was to say that the central office made those decisions: We had 128 lines in the budget that went to each building telling them exactly where they could spend their money. So, instead, we gave them a set amount of money for the year, all of which was discretionary. Your team or faculty made decisions as to the lines into which you wanted to allocate dollars. What programs do you want to support? Which ones do you think are not as important? We'll give you the flexibility of moving it around during the year if it doesn't work. Initially, teachers said they didn't want any part of this approach because they would have no one to blame if it didn't work. For example, if I don't get my travel allotment, I can't go to you and say, "Why didn't you give me the money?" or "That person withheld it." It took years to get the staff to feel comfortable with that level of decision making and that level of collaboration. It takes time. It doesn't just happen.

Emihovich: Your notion of trust is very important. I was able to go to the principal because he had been involved with BRIET for a long time. He had been with one of the schools that had committed to BRIET early on and was a very strong supporter. So you're right, it made it a lot easier. It would have been much more difficult to say those things to a principal that I didn't know very well or who didn't know the program very well. But I had to do it because we were hearing all these stories. Bob, you're right, it is an extreme case. Let me play devil's advocate with the example Jack just gave. Let's say you gave the money to a school and the school makes the decision to send 10 teachers to a conference, but the purpose of the conference was very suspect.

Helfrich: Sometimes I felt that many, many dollars were wasted in terms of conference attendance. So this is not an unusual occurrence. I would say that if there was consensus about the conference, then it was a good idea. If it was a bummer, we learned from it.

Jacobson: But, at least, that's the way you build trust within a two-way relationship.

Stevenson: Can I return to the issue of trust and time and what it means for the GSE? I look at these issues and I have a much more optimistic view of the changes that have taken place. I think that there has been a change in the trust between the university and the field. There is much more dialogue in public schools than there was before, and I think there is now more trust within the GSE.

Petrie: You really do have to spend the time to build that trust, and developing the necessary personal kinds of relationships takes time. You can't think of a curriculum as consisting of interchangeable parts. Suppose BRIET needs social foundations courses to be taught and we think of them as interchangeable among several faculty, some of whom can and some of whom cannot teach that course well. That is not very effective. What we need are faculty who understand not only social foundations but also what BRIET is trying do, or at least have a certain willingness to think about it, to see how other people are teaching within BRIET. I think this kind of collaboration needs to be a continual thing, and we cannot do that very well with existing structures. To be candid, one of the things that I had in mind from the beginning of our discussions of reorganization is that we needed to change the structure as a way of getting more of the kinds of interactions that we have been discussing. However, if we do not change the structure, then what other ways are there to encourage cross-departmental conversations? So the question becomes: What is occurring now that wasn't occurring before we had the planning effort?

Whether in the end the changes will be sufficient to meet the kinds of challenges to which we all referred in our chapters remains to be seen. The question is clear, I think, in Jack's and Catherine's chapters. How do you sustain these kinds of changes? If you are a little bit lucky and work hard and expect people to get going, you can get an initial burst of enthusiasm; you can see some results, and that does require a kind of personal level of trust. But, then people who did not participate in that first trust building have to be brought on board in some way or another. Individual trust is really important for the successes that you do have, but how do you get the next generation going? I don't know what the answer is.

If building trust is the first important step in changing relationships, the next important issue, as Helfrich and Petrie note, is finding ways to sustain commitment over the long haul. Our conversation now turns to some of the impediments to long-term commitment at the university. Suggestions are offered for structural and role changes, as well as changes in the ways we view research—changes that might help to support sustained commitment to particular schools on the part of faculty.

Emihovich: Last night at a meeting we were talking about the fact that Buffalo has a new superintendent and a lot of schools are going through changes and getting new personnel. We're discovering that we have to start doing some groundwork all over again. We have to begin to build a relationship with the new superintendent because he's not fully aware of what BRIET is. A couple of the associated schools that I told you about were committed to BRIET because the old superintendent was committed. I don't know what they're going to do. This is a dynamic, ongoing process. Which brings me back to the question: Are faculty prepared to commit for the long haul? There is a willingness on the part of my colleagues to get involved in schools, but I'm used to the field of anthropology. Anthropologists may be in the field for years, that's considered the norm. If you want to do this work in schools, you can't walk away after 6 months or a year. You have to think in terms of 5, maybe 10 years.

Helfrich: How do you develop staying power with a school as a faculty member of GSE? One of the things I argued for would be a joint appointment, so that a person could be in the school half-time and the university half-time. Then you see an organization in a different light, because you're a part of it. You have staying power because you are there, and that kind of relationship is different than when you are inserted and come out again. I think it will be great for schools if we could take advantage of the research knowledge of university faculty and, at the same time, they could understand that change takes time. There are a lot of things you can't do as an outsider, but you can if you're part of the district.

Emihovich: There are universities that have done that. Michigan State is a good example of where they have joint appointments. Some of the faculty spend a portion of their time teaching an actual class in a school, whether at the elementary or secondary level. I think that raises another dilemma within the faculty because the resource base for the university decreased by that amount that a person contributes to the school. Some are going to ask, "If we put a person half-time in a school, what are we gaining?" I'm not against the idea.

Stevenson: How does the university make up for that?

Petrie: Clearly, if you want to make joint appointments, you do need policy, and the university would somehow or another need to see work in the schools as useful. In research universities the first question would probably be What new kind of knowledge are you, in fact, going to discover in the schools. Any such knowledge would have to be peer reviewed and would likely be in the form of general laws which would be guide-lines for practice. So what we learn at UB, in fact, will make us very famous because other people can take these laws and apply them in other situations.

That, as you suggest in your chapter, Bob, is the dominant concep-tion of research. But most of us don't think that is the way educational research works. Certainly, I think Bob is arguing that it is the least effective model of research, yet this arts and sciences model of re-search resulting in general laws is still the overall paradigm for the university. So the task for schools of education within the university would be to argue that, however good the dominant model of research may be in some places, it is not appropriate for field-based educational research. In fact, we have other models of research and scholarship and service in the school of education which really are, in the end, important for the university. That's a tough sell, but not as much as it was 10 years ago because the modern university is more under attack by society and they are much less willing to buy esoteric research on faith.

I found this discussion very enlightening in helping me think about what else we need to work on. I think it is good that we haven't reached conclusion on some of these issues; they're not easily resolved. I would suggest that we have identified three main themes: Power is one, the nature of research is another; and change and resistance to change is the third. I like the idea of this conversation.

At this point our conversation begins to wind down. We now focus on our own activities within the GSE, and between the GSE and the field. It is clear that although all of the authors agree that significant changes have oc-curred, the pace of change is not fast enough for some. Perhaps of even greater importance than differences over the speed of change are differ-ences over the breadth of change that needs to occur within the faculty at the GSE. When Petrie poses the question of whether to support the initiatives of a small group of faculty, or insist that everyone get involved, the subsequent responses make clear differences that still need to be addressed among col-leagues who are trying to lead these changes.

Jacobson: I also like the idea of this conversation, but it strikes me as we talk that our work is still running in parallel.

Emihovich: I don't think so, not among us.

Jacobson: Yes, even among us! While we're interacting more with schools than in the past, and BRIET and LIFTS continue talking, our work hasn't crossed as much as I would have liked at this point.

Helfrich: One of my concerns is how do we keep trying to bridge the gap between the GSE and the schools. You asked what is to be gained by the schools or GSE. I think credibility, for one thing. You get a group of superintendents together and they never talk about the university. They talk about budgets and other things impinging on their lives, but they don't see the university as an important resource.

Stevenson: I think that is starting to change.

Helfrich: I think it is mainly because of what is being done by the people in this room, and I think that it is an important change that needs to take place. But how do we enhance it? What can we do to increase it?

Petrie: This may be a long-lasting dilemma. Do you just let the choir go ahead and sing their songs, because they're already converted and you're going to get interesting and good kinds of music? By the way, that is not bad. Or, do you want to insist that everybody get on exactly the same page? That isn't likely to work either.

Stevenson: I'm worried about us sounding that latter way in some of the chapters. I'm concerned that we have a bit of a self-righteous tone in that we come across as the only people who are really concerned about improving schools and we have the way to do it. That really worries me.

Emihovich: Well, there is some truth to that. I think you can have a broad mission that has many different pieces. However, from a resource standpoint, we cannot be all things to all people anymore. We are going to have to make some hard choices about how we're going to proceed. I don't mean this in a self-righteous sense. I just don't think we can afford the luxury of maintaining a large contingent of colleagues who say they don't have to have anything to do with the day-to-day realities of schools. Yes, they'll still be researching some issues related to education, but not the sort of messy and complex problems that will get their hands dirty. That is not going to be their thing, and I don't think we can afford the luxury of allowing that. Therefore, I will not support large numbers of people who think that way.

Stevenson: I don't think we have large numbers, especially with people retiring and most of the new faculty coming in with a new attitude.

Emihovich: But that's what will have to become the shift in emphasis.

Petrie: That's one of the implications of what you're talking about. Are we, in fact, going to use this kind of rhetoric? Has this kind of rhetoric of practice sufficiently infused what we do? Will we pick new faculty who want to do these new things?

Jacobson: Catherine, I like your "ready, fire, aim" approach. That's the way I like to operate, but I find at the university our approach is usually "ready, aim, aim."

Emihovich: Or, we rethink the target. Is this the target we want to have?

Petrie: Or, do we even want to get ready? That attitude has become very difficult for me. I wish I saw more evidence of the desire to change.

Helfrich: I see some kind of guerrilla warfare as necessary for a revolution to take place. Sooner or later it will become a revolution.

Stevenson: But, if too many more collaborative projects were happening, I would be worried that in some cases that may not be productive. I'm more cautious than you in the "ready, fire, aim" analogy because I see things rushed into which are counterproductive and may set us back.

Emihovich: That's why I use "ready, fire, aim." I learned from my first year at BRIET that things don't always work as planned. I had to go back and do some more groundwork. What I forgot is that when I brought the model up from Florida, I had already done a lot of groundwork there that I hadn't thought about doing here. I just said to myself, "Okay, I can put this model in, but the groundwork has to be laid again."

Petrie: That gets us back to the need for continuous change and continuous learning. It reminds me of a comment that Jack made. How do you renew the community or keep it going? It seems to me that the question is whether or not the process was well enough institutionalized in Ken-Ton to continue. That remains to be seen. This may be an argument for an emphasis on the process. If the process allows for the new people to build their own histories and to do their kinds of things, then you are not necessarily limited to the charismatic leader in the group that got it going the first time. Now everybody is working that process through and if they can go back to the process, they will have the possibility of again building the trust and again building the personal relationships, probably with a little bit of change, but also with the main goals and missions intact.

Helfrich: That's something we agree could be improved. I think that it is important. The other idea I'd add is that people who have different perceptions need to gather and talk. We need to promote that kind of ongoing development.

Stevenson: But Fullan also argues you have to stop and take stock of things. I think we've got to stop and be critical. That's what I see as part of the process, and probably where we have some differences, too.

Stevenson's comments provide a fitting conclusion for our conversation. This discussion and the chapters that preceded it allowed us the chance to stop and take stock critically of the change initiatives we have undertaken individually and collectively the past few years. It should be obvious that even among this small group of rather like-minded colleagues there are points of disagreement about changing the way we function as a graduate school of education. Although we are in general agreement about the need to improve the way we prepare educators and, in doing so, about the need to change the way we interact with the field, we have different perspectives about what changes will be required to achieve these goals and how these changes are to be implemented. But far more important than the fact that we have these differences is how we will choose to deal with them, both as a group and as a school of education.

Recall that toward the end of our conversation, we considered a few sequences of action needed for change that are variations on the "ready, aim, fire" theme. These variations include Fullan's notion of "ready, fire, aim," an approach that most of us endorsed, as well as two other approaches: "ready, aim, aim" and "ready, aim, rethink the target," calls to action we jokingly referred to as being more typical of university faculty. Just below the surface of our humor is the frustration that some of us have experienced when we feel that the faculty either cannot or will not "fire." To address our differences, we need to find an appropriate balance between our need for analysis and our need for action.

As we attempt to negotiate this balance, factors other than just our good intentions will also come into play. Helfrich and Emihovich both commented during the conversation on the dynamic, sometimes chaotic, nature of schools. Their observations are no less applicable to the GSE, and over the next few years we anticipate significant changes, especially in personnel, including the selection of a new dean, and a substantial number of faculty retirements and new hires. We will, undoubtedly, experience any number of unanticipated changes over the next few years as well. It is this constant flux, this interplay between intentional, anticipated, and random change, that will have the greatest influence on the kind of school of education we become. That said, we also believe that the continuing evolution of preparation programs such as BRIET and LIFTS, the development of our new Center for Continuing Professional Education, newly formed Holmes Partnerships with Buffalo State College and several area school districts, and other emerging field-based activities, such as the Collaborative Research Network, have set a course that is clearly placing school practice at the center of our school of education's work.

There are probably as many different ways to approach the kinds of changes discussed in this book as there are institutions attempting it. We certainly do not advocate our own approach as the best, especially because we're not entirely sure if it's even the best approach for us. Nevertheless, we know that our efforts over the past few years have had a direct effect on changing the way teachers and administrators are prepared at the GSE, as well as the way we approach our work with one another and our colleagues in the field. We believe that our efforts have also led other faculty to reexamine how schools and schools of education might work more collaboratively with one another. And, we hope that our efforts have encouraged others in the GSE not only to advocate reform, but to participate in the process itself.

As noted in the Introduction and Overview, although this book is about one school of education, we hope that the descriptions of our change efforts have served to illuminate significant issues presently confronting educational policymakers, practicing administrators, and university professors elsewhere. If we are to prepare high-quality educators to meet the challenges of tomorrow's schools, we must transform schools of education so that improving school practice is at the core of our collective work. Rather than attempting such a transformation in isolation, school by school, we believe it is important that we share our experiences and collective wisdom—offering for scrutiny our misgivings as well as our certainties, our differences as well as our agreement, and our failures as well as our successes. It is in that spirit that we offer this work, and we hope that our reflections prove useful to others embarking on this path.

CORWIN
PRESS

The Corwin Press logo — a raven striding across an open book —
represents the happy union of courage and learning. We are a profes-
sional-level publisher of books and journals for K–12 educators, and
we are committed to creating and providing resources that embody
these qualities. Corwin's motto is "Success for All Learners."